the **NO-NONSENSE** guide to

DEMOCRACY

Richard Swift

KT-437-551

VERSO

To my son, Josh.

About the author
Richard Swift is a co-editor with the **New Internationalist** magazine. He has worked in radio journalism and alternative publishing for many years and has a long-term interest in questions of ecology and democracy.

Acknowledgements
Special thanks to Larry Gordon, David Wallace, Jeremy Seabrook and especially Jonathan Barker for their invaluable comments on the text.

the **NO-NONSENSE** guide to

DEMOCRACY

Richard Swift

'Publishers have created lists of short books
that discuss the questions that your average
[electoral] candidate will only ever touch if
armed with a slogan and a soundbite. Together
[such books] hint at a resurgence of the grand
educational tradition... Closest to the hot
headline issues are *The No-Nonsense Guides*.
These target those topics that a large army of
voters care about, but that politicos evade.
Arguments, figures and documents combine to
prove that good journalism is far too important
to be left to (most) journalists.'

Boyd Tonkin,
The Independent,
London

The No-Nonsense Guide to Democracy
First published in the UK by
New Internationalist Publications Ltd
Oxford OX4 1BW, UK
www.newint.org

in association with
Verso
6 Meard Street
London
W1F 0EG
www.versobooks.com

Cover image: Ian Nixon

Design by New Internationalist Publications Ltd.
Production editor: Troth Wells

Printed by TJ International Ltd, Padstow, Cornwall, UK.

British Library Cataloguing-in-Publication Data.
A catalogue record for this book is available from the British Library.

Library of Congress Cataloguing-in-Publication Data.
A catalogue for this book is available from the Library of Congress.

ISBN 1-85984-470-7

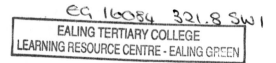

Foreword

ONE OF THE main themes of *The No-Nonsense Guide to Democracy* is Richard Swift's cogent argument that the free market – contrary to mainstream commonsense – is an anti-democratic force. Under the ideology of the free market, the market 'decides' vital social matters that in a democracy would be decided by the people. And not surprisingly, the free market *always* decides that some will get (stay) rich and others will get (stay) poor. Moreover, as the market image comes to permeate society as a whole, it begins to shape the political world as well, and citizens are transformed into 'consumers of politics', an audience for the antics of political superstars.

Globalization, Swift argues, carries this a step further. Decisions vitally affecting the lives of the people are taken out of the hands of the state (where the people had some chance of influencing them) and raised to the 'political stratosphere' of international trade and finance organizations (where the people had no chance of influencing them – until Seattle).

Globalization reproduces inequality in a different form, and simultaneously protects the privileged against its effects. The 'democratic' propertied class in the capitalist countries of the global North guard themselves against a 'vote against all property' by 'exporting' the most impoverished section of their working class to the global South. In this case, decisions that affect the lives of these workers are made in a different country, where under the nation-state system they have no voice – if indeed they have any political voice in their own countries, many of which are military or other forms of dictatorships. Of course this system is as old as colonialism; 'economic development' and 'globalization' are only its most recent incarnations.

Swift makes clear that 'democracy' is not the name of a system of government existing in certain countries, but rather the endpoint in a struggle that has a long way to go. If, as the End-of-Historyians say, with the demise of socialism, democracy is all there is, then fine, let's get down to it. Moreover, for a radical democrat like Swift, this does not mean simply tinkering with institutions or supplementing the list of human rights. A shift away from what he calls the 'strong market/weak democracy model' requires not only a change in institutions, but also a change in ethos, from the ethos of political consumerism to the ethos of citizenship. This possibility is not something that exists only in the realm of abstract theory, but is something that we see, at least in partial form, in daily life. Swift writes of the 'democratic outbreaks' that occur from time to time around the world, where people 'fly to assemblies' (Rousseau) and start taking matters into their own hands. He argues that there is a 'democratic impulse', a natural, commonsense desire to run one's own individual and community affairs, which exists everywhere, and is different from the 'democratic' ideology preached by the West. Democracy understood in this way can form the basis for understanding and solidarity among peoples who live in very different cultures, but who share the democratic impulse.

One of the very attractive things about this book is that it is written in democratic prose. So many democratic theorists make their writing inaccessible to the people they claim to be writing for, by writing in what amounts to code, which can only be decoded by a tiny inner circle of people around the world who have received their initiation in certain postgraduate institutions. How can one believe the democratic aspirations of such blatantly élitist writing? Swift's writing is straightforward and honest, with no escaping into unneeded abstraction or showing off with fashionable jargon. He says what he means, no more. That's how democrats should write.

C Douglas Lummis
Author of *Radical Democracy*

the NO-NONSENSE guide to
DEMOCRACY

CONTENTS

the **NO-NONSENSE** guide to

DEMOCRACY

AT THIS WRITING, the West's crusade against terrorism has launched its assault on the rubble of Afghanistan. This despite the warnings of everyone from the veteran British journalist Robert Fisk to the establishment US historian Arthur Schlesinger that the US led anti-terrorist alliance is falling into 'a sand trap' set for them by Osama Bin Laden. Indeed the reaction is already spreading throughout the Muslim world and shows every sign of escalating as the inevitable 'collateral damage' (the death of innocent civilians) rises. It is all somehow quite predictable. One could almost see, emblazoned across the south Manhattan skyline where the World Trade Center Towers once stood, the title of Benjamin Barber's prescient book *Jihad versus McWorld*.

But what about the rest of us? Those of us who reject a world dominated by unaccountable corporate power but are also appalled by fanatical terror and authoritarian programs of fundamentalism, Islamic or not. We are faced with a shrinking space in which to put forward any alternative. In an era of 'you are for us or against us' the language of absolutes (betrayal, loyalty, holy war, patriotism, crusade, jihad) is forcing out dissent of thought and deed.

And what of democracy? The new preoccupation is with security and sacrificing our liberties to safeguard our persons and property. The partisans of the national security state are gearing up to ever higher levels of surveillance of the citizenry, barricading the borders, and draining the coffers for ever more police and soldiers. Where is this taking us? The analogy of the US marine officer reporting back on military operations during the Vietnam War comes to mind: 'We had to destroy the village in order to save it.' Will we have to destroy democracy (even the limited version we have) in order to save it? Save it for what?

An alternative might be to look at the very fragile nature of what democracy we do have and try to figure out how to make it more robust. Neither McWorld nor Jihad have much use for democracy. To one it is a totem to be trotted out as a kind of ritual identification to rally the troops; for the other it is simply a Western subterfuge to cover amoral imperialist and materialist maneuverings. This is not surprising. A program of strong democracy would undo both fundamentalists and fund-managers. Neither the dictatorship of theocracy nor that of capital is compatible with the belief in democracy as the underlying principle for organizing society. This makes it our best hope.

So at a time when democratic space and principles are under attack from both McWorld and Jihad this *No-Nonsense Guide* is an attempt to help breathe life into the democratic possibility. Not the pale democracy of once-every-four-years marking your 'x' for some well-oiled political machine and its manicured candidate. But rather a democracy that exists on all levels of society. A democracy that roots itself in the everyday lives of fishers in India, traders in Kampala and workers in the Basque region of Spain. A democracy of the cities, the factories, the neighborhoods, even the world-system. A democracy that doesn't restrict itself to the higher reaches of the nation state. A democracy that goes back to the root of democratic meaning: self-rule.

Richard Swift
Toronto

1 What is democracy?

The recent confrontations over free trade have yielded some interesting juxtapositions over the meaning of democracy.

THE IRONY OF these juxtapositions came home to me amid the clouds of tear gas during the massive demonstrations against the extension of the current North American Free Trade Agreement (NAFTA) to include all 34 countries of the Americas but excluding Cuba. The Canadian Government decided to expropriate the center of Quebec City by slapping up a 4-kilometer fence to create a 'no-go' area to protect 'our' leaders from an unruly public. Over 6,000 police were marshalled from across the country to defend the fence against the thousands who gathered to protest the set of secret negotiations. The proposed Free Trade Zone of the Americas (FTAA) was designed around the notion of open markets and the rights of corporate investors. It assumed a particular model of 'let-the-market-decide' economic development. This model would squeeze out certain political and economic options – everything from a vibrant public sector to controls of speculative capital would in effect be ruled out. It thus significantly narrowed the democratic policy choices available to people throughout the hemisphere.

The conference agenda is by now a familiar one – deregulation, privatization, freedom for foreign investors, downsizing government. The 'free' in free trade is the tricky part. Free means democratic doesn't it? Not really. In effect our environmental and social rights were being traded away. No matter what we wanted as democratic citizens, corporate-inspired globalization is what we were going to get.

The battle of Quebec raged for three days. Tens of thousands rallied to say no to corporate globalization and put forward the idea that 'other Americas were possible'. The forces of order filled the old town with tear gas at a rate that peaked at 30 canisters a minute. Many Quebecois couldn't even stay in their own apartments. Hundreds were injured. Hundreds more were arrested, often on the most trivial of pretexts. The high point of the proceedings from an official point of view was the signing of a 'democracy clause' that committed all the leaders to maintaining elected civilian rule. It also achieved the US aim of isolating Cuba from the proceedings.

But this seemed to those of us on the other side of the fence a rather hollow definition of democracy. How could our leaders be meeting in secret to develop a program that would restrict our democratic rights and possibilities and still call it democracy? Did the word mean anything at all?

Is it enough, as the authorities claim, that politicians have democratic credentials (ie they were all in some way elected) to allow them to behave in an undemocratic manner? Is it the case, as many politicians believe, that once elected they can act as they choose as long as they aren't caught breaking any laws? Few of them had been elected on a mandate of trading away the rights of their citizens. Trade deals are for the most part not debated at election time. Instead, election campaigns mostly involve the usual set of vague commitments to good government and public order. Some even promised social justice and a narrowing of the gap between the rich and the poor. Many promised (although in fairness not George W Bush) a cleaner environment. Yet here they all were taking actions that would make these promises difficult if not impossible to keep. Was this democracy?

On the other side of the fence were the protesters. The corporate media was by-and-large hostile to this 'unallocated mob'. But in a democracy isn't it the role of citizens to take a vigilant interest in public affairs? When people see their rights stunted and diminished (indeed privatized) isn't it their democratic duty to rally to defend them? It felt like what the conference organizers really wanted was not active citizens at all. What they wanted felt more like consumers of 'good news' who would sit in front of their TV sets and nod enthusiastically at all the limos, photo ops and final communiqués.

The events in Quebec City raised for me questions about whether democracy is just about elections and voting every few years for someone who will then tell you what is best for you. Or does it have a wider definition? Is there buried in the history of democracy a more radical sense of citizens ruling themselves? If so, how have we managed to get so far away from that? And is it possible to get back?

When the demonstrators in Quebec breached the security fence I saw that as a victory for democracy. Those in power saw it as a violation of democratic law-and-order – an unwelcome interference with the democratic process. Will it ever be possible to bridge two such dramatically opposed visions of democracy?

2 Democratic malaise

'People who want to understand democracy should spend less time in the library with Aristotle and more time on the buses and in the subway.'

Simeon Strunsky, editor and essayist.

While democracy has triumphed as the political system of choice it is showing an increasing degree of popular disaffection. Voter turnout and other indicators of popular participation are in precipitous decline. The average citizen is feeling estranged from the political process and the more-or-less permanent political class that has come to dominate it. Money and those who control it easily shape the results of democratic decision-making. This is causing a crisis in the meaning of democracy although international surveys indicate that as a core social belief the majority still believes in democracy.

IT IS HARD to find anybody these days who doesn't believe in democracy. This was not always the case. Up until the mid-1800s, when movements for democratic rights began to grow in earnest, democracy was generally held to be a dangerous idea associated with barbaric mob rule that would likely destroy all civilized values if it ever caught on. And it was only very reluctantly (and after a hard, often violent struggle) that those without property were granted the full rights of citizenship. It was not until well into the 20th-century that the franchise was even extended to women. It was not until after World War Two that the colonized of Asia and Africa were considered 'mature' enough to decide their own fates.

But times have changed. Democracy or at least its mechanics are now the common currency of political life. It is meticulously studied in academic journals and university seminars. Journalists and pollsters build their careers sorting through the tea leaves to ascertain the underlying behavior of both voters and the politicians they elect. Almost all public policy debate is couched in terms of what people want/desire/need. Even dictators evoke a mysterious 'will of the people' to explain themselves. Not since 'the divine right of kings' has there been a significant political theory that was based on criteria in which democracy had no place. It would probably be just about possible to identify two openly antidemocratic strands of contemporary political thinking – religious fundamentalism of several stripes and technocratic authoritarianism. However in both these cases a significant part of the appeal is based on the notion that people need/desire (if they only imperfectly realize it themselves) the values embodied by a community of believers or the application of rigorous science to public policy.

Florida follies

But what is this democracy that we have all become so committed to? In the millennial year of 2000 the world was treated to an amusing (if somewhat disheartening) spectacle of two US Presidential candidates maneuvering to see who had actually won the national election. At stake was arguably the most important job in the world. Of the tens of millions of votes cast it boiled down to a few hundred votes in the state of Florida. This close contest hung on voting machines that didn't properly record the voter's intentions (particularly in poor areas), badly designed ballots that misled voters, police intimidation of some voters, the refusal by the highest court in the land to recount the vote, the exclusion of a significant portion of the electorate (mostly black) because they had (often trivial) criminal records, the use of vigilante mobs to stop the re-counting of ballots and the role of blatantly prejudiced authorities in adjudicating the outcome of the election. The result – a victory for Republican candidate

George W Bush through the vote of a winner-take-all Electoral College system that favors smaller often quite conservative states. He triumphed despite the fact he had received less of the popular vote than his Democratic challenger. This was not Zimbabwe or Haiti but the country which regards itself as the very heartland of democracy. Not some 'rogue nation' but the veritable international pulpit so often used to give finger-wagging sermons about glorious liberty and proper electoral conduct to the lesser races. The rest of the world could barely suppress its giggling. As could have been predicted the actual facts were blandly glossed over – the whole experience proving yet again (according to that dependable army of nation-boosters) the strength and resilience of American democracy. Eh? It recalled how the actor Peter Ustinov had once rather cruelly described democracy in the US as 'the inalienable right to sit on your own front porch in your pajamas, drinking a can of beer and shouting out "Where else is this possible?"'

This is not to say that there are not important movements for electoral reform in the US which would register more voters and arrange matters so that votes counted equally – through not only accurate methods of tabulation but also fair constituency boundaries. Controlling skyrocketing campaign spending is also crucial to US electoral reform strategies.

But almost as fascinating as the political shenanigans was the discourse of those seeking to manage and interpret events for the rest of us. It was as if the actual principles of democracy were less important than issues of stability, continuity and eventually 'closure'. Appearances needed to be kept up for the sake of the neighbors and the children. It had to be clear with as little doubt or delay (two things often necessary for democratic fairness) who was going to be at the 'helm' of global leadership. Otherwise it seemed the whole world might just crash and burn. Maintaining the facade of democracy was more important than its substance. How the stock market reacted, more important than how the people of Florida actually voted. It felt very much like a case of 'okay, we've gone through this vote ritual – now let's get back to what really matters'. This undoubtedly touched a chord with a near majority of the US electorate that have given up on the electoral process anyway. Even most opposition Democrats in the Gore camp wanted this mysterious closure, afraid perhaps that someone would shout – 'but the Emperor has no clothes'.

Democracy triumphant

Elsewhere, it seems, democrats have much to cheer about. Over the past 15 years it has been dictatorships rather than fragile democracies that have become the falling dominoes of Cold War mythology. Both military dictatorships and one-party state socialisms have been in dramatic retreat. Whether in the former Soviet republics of Asia or in the 'liberal' communisms of Eastern Europe, an autocratic state rule mired in economic malaise and under intense popular pressure, has folded like a proverbial house of cards. Even the most sinister *bêtes noires* of the Cold War – the Prussian Stalinism of East Germany and the mighty colossus in Moscow backed by the once ferocious Red Army – have been swept away by 'people's power' revolutions. They have been replaced by a series of regimes with claims to at least some kind of political pluralism. Only the rest of Asian communism and the isolated little island of Cuba remain bastions of one-party communist rule.

In Latin America the military has been forced back to the barracks in country after country particularly in the Southern Cone, although countries like Venezuela and Colombia still suffer from significant militarization. The latter remains the last major beneficiary of the kind of US military aid and training programs (part of the seemingly endless War on Drugs) that helped keep the continent under a reign of military

Electoral democracies

As of January 2000, electoral democracies represent 120 of the 192 existing countries and constitute about 60 per cent of the world's population.

List of Electoral Democracies (120) as of January 2000

Albania	Guatemala	Nigeria
Andorra	Guinea-Bissau	Norway
Argentina	Guyana	Palau
Armenia	Haiti	Panama
Australia	Honduras	Papua New Guinea
Austria	Hungary	Paraguay
Bahamas	Iceland	Philippines
Bangladesh	India	Poland
Barbados	Indonesia	Portugal
Belgium	Ireland	Romania
Belize	Israel	Russia
Benin	Italy	St Kitts and Nevis
Bolivia	Jamaica	St Lucia
Botswana	Japan	St Vincent and the
Brazil	Kiribati	Grenadines
Bulgaria	Korea, South	Samoa
Canada	Kyrgyzstan	San Marino
Cape Verde	Latvia	São Tomé and
Central African	Liberia	Príncipe
Republic	Liechtenstein	Senegal
Chile	Lithuania	Seychelles
Colombia	Luxembourg	Slovakia
Costa Rica	Macedonia	Solomon Islands
Croatia	Madagascar	South Africa
Cyprus	Malawi	Spain
Czech Republic	Mali	Sri Lanka
Denmark	Malta	Suriname
Djibouti	Marshall Islands	Sweden
Dominica	Mauritius	Switzerland
Dominican Republic	Micronesia	Taiwan
Ecuador	Moldova	Thailand
El Salvador	Monaco	Trinidad and Tobago
Estonia	Mongolia	Turkey
Fiji	Mozambique	Tuvalu
Finland	Namibia	Ukraine
France	Nauru	United Kingdom
Georgia	Nepal	United States of
Germany	Netherlands	America
Ghana	New Zealand	Uruguay
Greece	Nicaragua	Vanuatu
Grenada	Niger	Venezuela

Democracy's Century, Freedom House www.freedomhouse.org

terror for decades. For years the US has trained the officer corps of Latin America at the Georgia-based School of the Americas to fight against the Left. It was a stretch to see the techniques of interrogation, torture and political manipulation as having anything to do with democracy. But this was an era of Cold War ends justifying a wide variety of anti-democratic means. An era when then US senior 'statesman' Henry Kissinger could justify US support for the bloody coup that brought down Chilean democracy – 'I won't see a country go Communist because of the irresponsibility of its people.'

But today things are different. The undignified retreat to Japan of autocratic President Fujimori of Peru, the defeat of the almost century-long PRI Party's control of Mexican political life and the noble attempts to hold the former Chilean dictator Augusto Pinochet accountable for his crimes are all signs of a real enough democratic vitality.

Even in Africa, home of an often bloated and highly militarized post-colonial state, there are some hopeful signs – the defeat of apartheid in South Africa and the first relatively honest elections for many years in the continent's most populous country, Nigeria. It is a promising start, but otherwise representative government only clings on in a few countries of West (Ghana, Senegal) and southern (Botswana, Mozambique and Malawi) Africa. The North, East and the Horn regions are still preyed on by political bosses who would rather fight than switch – Moi in Kenya and the Bashir Government in Sudan being amongst the most recalcitrant.

Elsewhere the good news just keeps coming with a belated people's revolt in Serbia finally getting rid of one of the cruder forms of Balkan nationalism with the dismissal of the Slobodan Milosevic regime; and the overthrow of the Suharto regime in Indonesia. Only the brutal military regime in Burma and a military seizure of power in Pakistan, that holds a restive population of some 130 million under its sway, blot the democratic landscape.

There are many other signs of an emerging international consensus on the value of representative institutions and respect for at least a minimum of human rights. The World Bank and the International Monetary Fund (IMF) are proposing to punish those whose records on things like 'transparency' and 'good governance' are deemed to be inadequate. This is a far cry from the days when political and economic stability were the flavor of the month and these two erstwhile champions of democracy turned a blind eye to the corpses in the national stadium in Chile or Indonesia's rivers of blood following the military coup of 1967. In both cases the overthrow of left-leaning civilian rule was seen as the preferable option for the geopolitical interests of the Cold Warriors who ran these institutions. This marks a major change. The end of Cold War competition should have taken a lot of the ideological heat and hypocritical posturing out of political debate. There should be a welcome clearing of the air and return to more honest criteria over 'what is' and 'what isn't' democracy. The Cold War led to some very cynical hypocrisies: one striking example being the demonizing of the Sandinista Government in Nicaragua (despite the Sandinistas' surrender of power when they were defeated at the polls) while vicious dictatorships from Cape Town to Caracas got lionized as bulwarks of a supposedly 'free world'. On the Soviet side many countries with dubious socialist credentials – one thinks of the brutal dictatorship of General Mengistu in Ethiopia – were similarly championed.

Democracy after the Cold War

With the end of the Cold War it is no longer enough to have to justify a set of political arrangements (whether democratic or not) by reference to an undemocratic and sinister 'other' by simply saying 'things could be a lot worse'. Now democracy or its absence must stand naked on its own and be judged for what it is rather than what it isn't. And it is not just the intelligentsia of politics (political scientists, journalists, pundits and so on) who are now doing this but also ordinary citizens. The results of such judgements are quite sobering. For if democracy appears on the one hand never stronger, it is also being subjected to a groundswell of dissatisfaction from below.

The indicators of this dissatisfaction are everywhere. The decline in voter participation has spread beyond North America (in the US less than 50 per cent of the electorate bothers to vote and the last Canadian elections witnessed the lowest turnout in the country's history). Most non-compulsory European voter participation has dropped significantly over the past 20 years. A study of 15 Western European countries found that membership in political parties had declined almost a third from 8.2 per cent of the electorate in the early 1980s to 5.2 per cent by the mid-1990s.[1] To take just one graphic example, the British Conservative Party – once one of the largest political parties in the world with three million members after the Second World War has now barely a tenth of that number.

You can almost taste the disappointment with democracy in Eastern Europe and the countries that made up the former USSR. The same old figures who ran things under the old communist system are now often back dressed in democratic clothes. The electorate swings erratically between Left and Right looking for the elusive promise of democracy. The old cynicism from below that marked communist rule is now reborn as a reaction to the new political élite that is consolidating power.

Public opinion data from Latin America is also revealing. The proportion of those who feel dissatisfied with democracy ranged from 40 per cent in Peru and Bolivia to 59 per cent in Brazil and 62 per cent in

Colombia.[2] Everywhere it is the economically marginal, those with less resources (and arguably more to gain from responsive government) who are absenting themselves from the political process.

In the UK for example only 2.6 per cent of those who own property are not on the electoral register while 38.2 per cent of those living in furnished rental accommodation have never bothered to register.[3] Democratic politics is becoming more a means for the relatively privileged to defend what they have, rather than a vehicle for a more equal vision of society.

Frustrated voters

Even where people still bother to cast their ballots they find the political arrangements in place limit their influence and frustrate their intentions. Systems based on the Westminster 'first-past-the-post' (FPTP) model (peculiar to the English-speaking world) are particularly bad at reflecting the broad range of political opinions and options. Voters are often caught in the 'lesser-of-two-evils' syndrome. FPTP tends to group a couple of large well-funded parties with fairly similar ideologies (in practice if not in rhetoric) which reinforces the general public perception that politicians are 'all the same'. These parties are often referred to as 'brokerage parties' because of their 'all things to all people' approach during election campaigns and their lack of commitment to any clear ideology beyond the pragmatism of power. They bring whatever interests are available into some kind of working arrangement so that getting a piece of the action *is* the ideology. Extreme views, populist impulses, new thinking and idiosyncratic figures are all casualties of a bland sameness that pervades political culture. Theirs is a muscular orthodoxy that reinforces this by actively marginalizing outlying ideas. Oddly this sameness does not lead to civility in political life: for where real policy differences are absent, politics tends to revolve around personality and endless expensive attempts at proving what a lowlife scoundrel the other guy is. This has been dubbed the silly season of politics that often immediately precedes an election.

While there is also a tendency towards this in voting systems based on proportionality (Proportional Representation or PR is the main system of electoral representation in Europe, Latin America and the former Soviet Union) it is far more pronounced under FPTP. Voter turnout is lower and voter dissatisfaction higher under FPTP. Little wonder when a political party can win a 'landslide' mandate with the votes of only forty-odd per cent of those who even bother voting, depending how the vote splits.

Another way voters find their preferences frustrated is in boundary arrangements that privilege some voters over others. Sometimes this is the result of gerrymandering – the manipulation of political boundaries by the ruling party to gain the best possible results. More typically this situation favors rural voters over their urban counterparts. For example in Canada there are some 101 seats (mostly urban) with between 100,000 and 120,000 citizens while 35 others (mostly rural) are decided by 20,000 to 75,000 voters[4]. A rural tilt to voting can exercise a conservative influence on political life – clearly seen in countries like France or Germany or in the US where senators from sparsely-populated western states ensure the defeat of many otherwise popular environmental protection measures.

The conscious exclusion of certain categories of potential voters militates against a really inclusive democracy. While a franchise based on property-holding has fallen out of favor there are still many categories of exclusion. Migrant workers are excluded almost everywhere and this is particularly unfair as in parts of Europe they form a significant percentage of the working class and have lived in their 'host' societies for decades. People with criminal records are excluded from voting in some places including many parts of the US. Since the US imprisons a large percentage of its black male population, this in effect becomes a category of racial exclusion. In those places with elaborate voter registration systems, it is often difficult for the poor and semi-literate to vote. The political rights of women from Sudan to Afghanistan are severely curtailed.

In many cases it is not the lack of the opportunity to vote that is the problem. In the US alone there are estimated to be an astounding 500,000 public officials who need to get elected. Other democracies with hidebound civil service bureaucracies might consider making more positions, particularly local positions, elected ones. But the main predicament facing most democracies is people who exclude themselves from

Women in Parliament

In Brunei, UAE, Qatar, Saudi Arabia, Oman and Kuwait, women's right to vote and stand for election has not been recognized. In Switzerland, women only received the right to vote in 1971; in New Zealand it was granted in 1893.

	% Women in Lower House 1999	% Women in Ministerial posts 1998
Aotearoa/New Zealand	29	8
Australia	22	17
Canada	21	n/a
China	22	n/a
Cuba	28	5
Czech Republic	15	17
Iran	5	0
Mexico	17	5
Mozambique	25	0
Norway	36	20
South Africa	30	n/a
Thailand	6	4
Uganda	18	13
UK	18	24
US	13	26
World average	11	n/a

The World's Women 2000, United Nations;
UN Human Development Report 2001, UN/OUP.

electing candidates. This reflects widely-held feelings of apathy and powerlessness. The politicians who are supposed to represent people are often considered distant and unresponsive. They are a class apart from the normal voter. If there is either no contest (one candidate is deemed to be unbeatable) or no significant issue (all candidates support variations of the same policy) this voter apathy is bound to skyrocket.

A study done by US-based Center for Voting and Democracy analyzed a series of Congressional elections and found that voter participation varied between 30 per cent (no contest) and 43 per cent (close call) depending on the competitiveness of the race[5]. So voter participation would be enhanced in contentious elections where there are significant philosophical differences between candidates. Is it surprising then that in most of the industrial world, where politicians cling to a narrow range of views on the fundamentals of how to run a market economy (privatization, cuts in spending and in taxes, deregulation, incentives to wealthy investors) that so many voters just can't be bothered?

A professional political class

But democracy's malaise goes deeper than the decline in voting and the manipulation of electoral arrangements by a self-serving élite. It stems from the very depths of what we imagine democracy to be. Many still have the lingering sense that democracy means 'rule by the people' – in other words, people participate in the decisions that affect them most closely. If this is the central criterion of a democracy, we are a long way from it now. This sense of a failed promise to actually achieve a democratic life is perhaps the underlying reason for the groundswell of discontent.

Our current systems of democracy – highly centralized governments in which we are 'represented' by a class of professional politicians – seem to have betrayed the promise of self-rule. And while the lack of real choice in competitive candidates and ideas amongst these professional politicians is a part of the malaise, it is hardly the whole picture. The system of centralized state power seems increasingly remote from most people's lives and it becomes difficult to believe that politicians (no matter what their views) concerned with the macro-management of society and economy have any real interest in what is important to us.

This view is reinforced every time a politician tells voters one thing to get elected (they will remove a particular tax, not sign a trade agreement, bring in a new social program) and when they are in power does the exact opposite. While this is often put down to the typical hypocrisy of politicians, it is more than that. It is a go-with-the-flow, do-what-powerful-business-interests-want and don't-rock-the-boat kind of ethos that glues political life together.

A consequence of this is an extraordinary popular hostility to not only the political class but government per se and all its works. Conservative politicians have proved the most adept at harnessing this hostility (often glorifying the 'honest' market at the expense of the 'corrupt' state) and using anti-government rhetoric to achieve, paradoxically, the very positions of power they are attacking. They are even prone to attack 'big government' at the same time they are cynically using the powers of the state to reward their friends and vanquish their enemies. Juxtaposing the 'choice' offered by the market (with the important caveat that you have the money to exercise this choice) with the lack of any real political choice contributes to the democratic malaise. It is a deceptive sleight-of-hand that portrays the market

---

No chance to vote

Brunei Darussalem, Oman, Qatar and Saudi Arabia have never had a parliament.

UN Human Development Report 2001, UN/OUP.

as a mechanism of or for democracy. But in a situation of democratic disappointment and alienation from an unaccountable political class the wizardry often goes unnoticed.

The centralization of political power is at work on almost all levels – whatever the champions of the market would have us believe. The big political parties are increasingly remote from the voters. Members of the parties in convention see their policy resolutions routinely ignored by those they help elect. The rank-and-file backbench representative who sits in a parliament or national assembly has little control over the cabinet, or if in opposition the shadow cabinet. The cabinet has less control over the increasingly large office of the chief executive, be they Prime Minister, President or Premier. 'Don't tie our hands' is the cry used all down the line to drown out the sound of breaking promises and abandoned commitments.

We are left with a series of puzzling questions as to why government isn't better at representing the public interest and who is really setting the agenda.

Who gets to the top?

The kind of people who have already accumulated a high level of economic and social power are usually over-represented in the political class. Lawyers and those from the corporate boardroom tend to predominate. Other professionals are not far behind. It is really the 'better sort of people'.

Groups that are on the 'outs' – blacks in the US, *Dalits* ('untouchables') in India, many types of immigrants, tribal peoples everywhere – tend to be greatly under-represented. Women have traditionally been excluded and although there is some change here (particularly in Northern Europe and to a lesser degree South Asia and South Africa) they are also grossly under-represented. Women still make up less than 15 per cent of the members of representative assemblies around the world and the figure drops to well below 10 per cent when it comes to government posts and cabinet-level positions[6].

This political class forms a more or less permanent – if sometimes rotating – government élite. The same faces pop up over and over again. The frequency with which we hear about the phenomenon of the 'political comeback' is a good indicator of how difficult it is to get rid of them. Former military politicians like Hugo Banzer in Bolivia or Rios Montt in Guatemala rebound into public prominence. Their careers in 'public service' span decades. Sometimes a figure will serve many political masters and blow with the ideological breezes, shifting gracefully from Left to Right (and sometimes even back again). Perhaps in no other human endeavor is the octogenarian male so prominent. Men in their late 70s and early 80s play a disproportionate role in the governing of many nations. The US at the time of writing has a senator – Strom Thurmond – who is over 100 years old.

A certain species of celebrity can even attach itself to the more charismatic figures. Show-business figures (Reagan in the US, Estrada in the Philippines) or former monarchs like the ex-king of Bulgaria are good raw material for politics because they have already been touched by celebrity. As with most celebrities these are magical figures who exist in a realm different from our own. The most important ones are surrounded by a security apparatus to ensure they remain untouchable. Security for the powerful has become both an obsession and a multi-billion dollar business. We are supposed to feel grateful when one of them does a 'streeter' mixing with the crowds and displaying that carefully-crafted 'common touch' that is so important for professional politicians to cultivate. The recurrence of the same family names speaks to the continuity in the political class – Kennedy, Bush, Bhutto, Clinton, Churchill and Gandhi.

Politicians from this governing culture tend to form a seamless web with those who hold power in the economy and society more generally. They are on the same boards, live in the same toney neighborhoods, are members of the same clubs, have their kids in the same private schools. It is by-and-large a comfortable world although the pressures of hanging on can be very real. There is a shared ethos of doing things 'properly' – which usually means doing things in ways that do not threaten and if possible enhance the interests of that world.

Vice-president Dick Cheney in the Bush administration is a classic example. Cheney is a long-time member of the conservative wing of the US political class who served as Secretary of Defense under Bush senior in the early 1990s. He then moved into private business – a big Dallas-based oil services company called Halliburton. When he first started at Halliburton they were doing less than $300 million of work for the US Defense Department. When he left it was up over $650 million. Paul O'Neill, Treasury Secretary in the Bush cabinet, and the former chair of Alcoa (the world's largest aluminum company) apparently felt no need to divest himself of his $90 million-plus stock options in that company. In Russia the business-cum-criminal class of wealthy oligarchs formed a kind court around Boris Yeltsin and now Vladimir Putin. In Italy Silvio Berlusconi, one of the country's richest men, who has a stranglehold on much of the Italian media, has used his wealth and influence to make himself one of the leading figures in Italian politics. A kind of 'revolving door' often operates between the political and economic élites, rewarding the former for their services once they leave office. In the South the difference between the circumstances of the political class and that of the ordinary citizenry is even more marked. Their money is often in places where wealth seeks asylum (Switzerland or the Cayman Islands), their children in universities in Australia and the US, their healthcare in Singapore, Europe or America and their property in Paris or California.

Crooked politicians

A revealing way in which politicians have become 'a class apart' is in their belief almost across the political spectrum that they stand *legibus solitus* or 'above the law'. Whether it was a matter of illegal wiretapping (Mitterand) or municipal rake-offs (Chirac), personal enrichment (Yeltsin and Salinas) or evasion of democratic accountability (Reagan in the Iran/Contra affair), the political class consistently breaks the law for reasons of financial gain or to maintain and protect its own power.

They are often not caught and seldom prosecuted. Two graphic exceptions are President Joseph Estrada of the Philippines caught pilfering the public coffers and President Carlos Menem of Argentina indicted for illegal arms sales. But often a public apology seems to suffice. In many places, such as Japan, such apologies have become a kind of national rite. The 'sacred trust' of elected office is now almost constantly beset by scandal from Peru to Poland. The arrogance of power resides in the unstated but persistent conviction that the 'divine right of kings' has been modified into a kind of 'divine right of elected leaders'.

Another source of popular alienation to the way democracy is currently practised has to do with money. There is a pervading sense that money makes democracy dirty. It is estimated that the last US presidential election cost approximately one billion US dollars. Major contributors are seen to be in a good position to exert influence on those whom they help elect. For example the tobacco giant Philip Morris is one of the largest contributors in the US[7]. It seems unlikely that this does not buy a certain amount of access and influence.

As party membership declines, politicians must depend more and more on corporate largesse to fund expensive media-based advertising campaigns during elections. The UK Labour Party is a classic case. As the donations of individual donors recede in importance, major corporate donors are filling the gap. This includes everybody from the US fast-food chain McDonald's to Lords Hamlyn and Sainsbury (of supermarket chain fame) who each coughed up £2,000,000 ($2.8 million). In April 2000, the Party held a £500-a-plate ($700) dinner where major companies with important stakes in government decisions gobbled up most of the gourmet goodies at the Grosvenor Hotel.

The increasingly large amounts of money needed to achieve electoral success flies in the face of conventional US democratic mythology which holds that a person is supposed to be able to move 'from log cabin (or trailer park) to White House'. At such prices this appears about as likely as the rest of the fairy tales about people moving from 'rags to riches' by picking themselves up by their own bootstraps. That competing nostrum of common sense that 'the rich get richer and the poor get poorer' comes a lot closer to most people's experience.

Money still talks

Various remedies have been proposed and implemented to level the political playing field so that money does not have such a large say. Most of this has been in the form of spending limits and other campaign finance legislation. Such limits have, by and large, been weaker in North America and stronger in their restrictions in Europe and elsewhere. Since this kind of legislation came into effect virtually every major democracy (and a few smaller ones as well) has been rocked by revelations of lawbreaking to avoid campaign finance rules by some major political figure. The best known case is that of Helmut Kohl, the long-time conservative Chancellor of Germany, who laundered a fortune in illegal campaign contributions and sank the political fortunes of his Christian Democratic Party. But it does not stop there: campaign finance scandals rocked the Clinton administration in Washington and are almost a monthly occurrence in

Japan. In Britain New Labour has recently come under attack for its economic dependence on a few key billionaires. Politicians everywhere are caught in the dilemma of how to raise the big bucks needed for political success without appearing to be in the back pocket of wealthy contributors. Campaign finance controls spring from an understandable desire for honesty and fairness. The consistent breaking or evasion of these rules is yet another source of the growing alienation from the dominant political class.

What all this campaign money sloshing around does is buy a lot of 'image'. The elaborate machinery of electoral success (pollsters, focus groups, telemarketers, saturation advertising, brain trusts of consultants, hoopla political conventions) have been exported from the US along with Disney movies and Microsoft computer games. The same voters who are alienated by big money politics may be seduced by the image that it buys. Policy and issues of substance shrink in political importance, overshadowed by competing image-machines playing on the personal virtues of leaders – strength, integrity and so on. A classic proof is a directive leaked by a British Labour Party MP which came from the Party leadership in the run-up to a national election. The 'good members' were told to spend a maximum of 30 seconds talking to their constituents and that they should not engage in prolonged discussion with anyone about Party policy. So much for representation and sober reflection. Turbo-capitalism is throwing up a politics whose democracy is a matter of show-business that has abandoned any real interest in popular sovereignty.

Uploading power

Centralization of power into the hands of a narrow political élite doesn't just take place within political parties or national governments. It is happening at all levels of governance. Centralization is sucking the vitality from regional, municipal and local government where their powers (particularly over the raising of money through taxation) are being usurped by national politicians. Thus the levels of government closest to people are left with the least power to shape policy and defend the quality of life. They often have no constitutional existence of their own, instead owing their legal arrangements to the whim of governments 'above' them. Such 'superior' governments think nothing of intervening to change electoral arrangements, eliminate mayors, redraw municipal boundaries and even eliminate whole levels of government. Power is often reduced while responsibilities are increased. The term 'downloading' has been coined to describe the phenomenon of the national state shedding responsibilities – but rarely the resources needed to meet them – to local levels of government. Local government is a key provider of many popular government services (recreation, public space, welfare, local environment, local policing, much of public health, housing and homelessness, education in some places) while national states retain the bulk of the resources to fund national programs and the trappings of state (the security apparatus, the foreign service, and the elaborate protocol machine). It is not hard to figure out in this dynamic of centralization where programs are most vulnerable to cost-cutting measures.

As if this wasn't enough, even nation-states are now subjected to pressures from institutions buttressed almost entirely from public democratic pressure; institutions such as the International Monetary Fund (IMF) and the World Trade Organization (WTO). These are the semi-official bodies that enforce the shifting rules of the globalizing economy. The concentration of power in their hands and that of private actors in the global economy (transnational corporations, capital markets, stockholders, currency speculators, bond-rating agencies) has led to an explosion of social science literature pondering the future of the nation-state. This literature tries (from widely differing points of view) to come to terms with a world in which the once sacrosanct sovereignty of (at least powerful) nation-states is now being hemmed in by economic forces that severely limit economic policy choices.

Nor are restrictions limited to purely economic matters. Such things as government-supported health policies, workplace health and safety, public support for the arts and environmental safeguards all potentially come under a regime of international trade regulations adjudicated and enforced outside the parameters of national legislation. In practical terms this could result in public policy (say outlawing a polluting additive in gasoline or support for domestic film production) that was publicly supported by the vast majority of citizens but overruled because it does not fit with a series of international trade and investment rules.

The implications for even the limited amount of democratic choice we still have are obvious enough. The rules are by-and-large ones that favor market solutions (rather than, say, public investment or a government-supported cooperative sector) and the interests of transnational corporations. In other words they empower individual and corporate efforts to maximize private incomes and profits and rule out our collective discussion and decision about the kind of cities, towns and societies we live in.

The opinions in the flood of writing on 'the crisis of the nation-state' stretch from those who celebrate the much-needed discipline the wholesome market imposes on 'unrealistic' democratic aspirations to those appalled by the threat to popular sovereignty. Different theorists give different weightings to this 'drag effect' of globalization on the public policy decisions of supposedly sovereign governments; none however dispute its existence or its continued growth.

In conclusion it is fair to say that representative institutions are becoming (with important exceptions) the norm in various parts of the world. But at the same time there is a growing citizen alienation with the 'actually-existing democracies'. This is in part due to the tendencies towards political élitism and manipulation built into the conventional practice of politics. It is in part due to a centralization that sucks power from the local into ever less accountable realms of the political stratosphere, realms that sometimes seem to move beyond the reach of politics altogether. The alienation has a positive side however: it means there is a lingering sense that democracy could and should be more. The rest of this book will endeavor to explain how we arrived at this tepid commitment to democracy and evaluate the potentials for a more robust version.

1 *1999 Democracy Forum Report*, Institute for Democracy and Electoral Assistance, Stockholm. **2** 'State Decay and Democratic Decadence in Latin America', Atilio Boron, *Socialist Register* 1999, Merlin Press Sussex. **3** *Democratic Audit*, Charter 88, London 1997. **4** Democracy Watch, Ottawa. **5** 'This Time Let the Voters Decide', Rob Richie and Steven Hill, in *Making Every Vote Count*, ed Henry Milner, Broadview Press, Peterborough 1999. **6** Inter-Parliamentary Union and the UN Division for the Advancement of Women. **7** *Multinational Monitor*, March 2000.

3 Weak and strong democracy

'In democracy you can be respected though poor, but don't count on it.'

Charles Merrill Smith, writer.

Two strains can be identified in the history of democratic thought and experience. One is a weak democracy where popular sovereignty is hemmed in by the individual right to property that holds sway over the collective rights of the community. This theory is based on a notion of possessive individualism and is a strong market/weak democracy model. The second strain is the notion of strong democracy rooted in the radical republican tradition which emphasizes the self-rule of the political community and the equality of power in democratic decision-making.

EVEN AT DEMOCRACY'S birth, its critics were present and vocal. Plato and Socrates greeted its appearance in ancient Athens with grave warnings about entrusting the well-being of the city to an unpredictable mob. Both opposed the direct involvement of the whole body of citizens in its own self-government. Instead they preferred a politics firmly in the grip of the better sort, experts in the specific knowledge of politics (ie today's political class). Athenian democracy (a direct democracy of rich and poor alike but excluding women and slaves) had its champions as well. Protagoras, a friend and advisor to the influential Pericles, held that any adult citizen was capable of acquiring the art of politics (the ability to make reasoned judgements on the city's affairs) and should therefore be part of the body deciding these issues. Even Aristotle, another critic of full democracy, thought that a person became fully human only by taking part in politics. The Greek notion of the 'idiot' meant someone ignorant of public affairs.

Thousands of Athenian citizens would gather to debate and decide on the issues of the day.

As democratic activist/theorist Douglas Lummis points out, 'while the Athenians did not invent slavery and patriarchy (or empire for that matter), neither did they abolish them; what they did do was to discover public freedom'[1]. Looking back from the 19th century the political philosopher John Stuart Mill held that the Athenian achievement of a substantial degree of citizen self-government 'raised the intellectual standards of an average Athenian citizen far beyond anything of which there is yet an example in any other mass of men, ancient or modern'[2].

After the collapse of the Athenian and later the Roman Republics the intellectual debate as to the merits of democracy faded. But this did not curtail people's efforts to control their own circumstances and fate. The democratic impulse has been widespread across time and place – taking a multitude of forms in different early societies, and religious movements, artisan guilds, monastic communities and in a rich variety of peasant revolts. Heretical sects, such as the Albigensians or Cathars in the south of France and the dissenting movements of Eastern Europe resisted the power of both the central Church and State. The democratic impulse both predates and coexists with more elaborated theories of democracy and acts as a constant pressure to push the limits of 'actually existing democracies' in both theory and practice.

This democratic impulse cannot be claimed by the West in the way it claims the formal liberal-democratic tradition rooted in the philosophy of the Enlightenment and the practice of the American and French Revolutions. It is more widely cast in the struggles of peasant villages against landlords and warlords, tribal peoples against enemies of an egalitarian way of life, independent peoples against expanding empires, religious dissenters against power-wielding clerics and even the rebellions of youth against domination by elders.

Anthropologists disagree as to when, where and why a power separate from society crystallized in the form of a hierarchy. But perhaps a buried memory of a time before state and kingship is the original source of the democratic impulse.

Possessive individualism

Thinking about democracy as a system of government that is a contract between ruler and ruled starts to emerge only in the 16th and 17th centuries. But these theorists of a government based on the consent (of at least some) of the governed – the Hobbes, Mills, Lockes, even the more radical Rousseaus and Jeffersons – were also deeply ambivalent about the foundational meaning of democracy, ie 'rule by the people'. In the original Greek, democracy is the *kratos* of the *demos* – the power of the people. But by the 17th century this had to be reconciled with a large number of anti-democratic structures: monarchies, aristocracies, slavery, patriarchy and the emergence of a class of wealthy property owners. The dreamers of the new democratic freedom were almost all haunted by nightmares of 'mob rule' and the overthrow of property. As Ireton, the Roundhead leader Cromwell's right-hand man, cautioned the uppity Levellers, who had been inspired by the ideals of the English Revolution to want a more profound democracy, 'liberty cannot be provided for in a general sense if property is (to be) preserved'.

So the original thinkers and theorists of a liberal democracy drew back from the precipice and judged that only men with a certain amount of property could be trusted with the exercise of consent (the vote). This limited notion of a liberal democracy, particularly associated with John Locke and James Mills, has been dubbed by the political philosopher CB Macpherson as a 'theory of possessive individualism'. Those without property are seen by definition as irresponsible (lacking a stake in society) and thus had to be excluded

Democracy timeline

The table below depicts the major events throughout ancient and modern history that helped shape the development and spread of democracy. From the Ten Commandments to the founding of the first university, Gutenberg's printing press and the creation of the Internet, all have served to further and strengthen the democratic system.

18thC BC	Hammurabi establishes first legal code
16-13thC	The Ten Commandments revealed to Moses on Mount Sinai
212 AD	"Civis Romanus sum" citizenship is given to freeborn subjects
221	Han Dynasty in China includes official, but diverse news circulation
600	Book printing is invented in China
701	Codification of Japanese political law
790	Golden period of Arabic learning
802	Germanic tribal laws codified by order of Charlemagne
970s	Fatimids build al-Azhar University in Cairo, the world's first university
1119	Bologna University founded in Italy; Paris University, in France, is founded in 1150
1215	King John seals Magna Carta at Runnymede
1455	Gutenberg invents movable-type printing press
1492	Christopher Columbus lands in the Caribbean (beginning of European expansion)
1517	Martin Luther publishes 95 theses, launching the Reformation in Europe
1619	First representative colonial assembly in America
1625	Hugo Grotius publishes *De Jure Belli ac Pacis*, which becomes the basis of international law
1646	Treaty of Westphalia: End of the Thirty Years' War in Europe; Ushers in modern concept of the nation-state
1679	Habeas Corpus Act in England ensures no imprisonment without court appearance first
1689	Act of Toleration and Bill of Rights is passed in England
18thC	Age of Enlightenment begins in Europe
1762	Jean-Jacques Rousseau writes *The Social Contract*. He asserts that if a government fails to serve its subjects well, they should have the right to overthrow it and create a new one
1775	Beginning of the American Revolution
1776	Adam Smith writes *Wealth of Nations*
1776	The United States declares independence
1787	The American Constitution and Bill of Rights established
1789	The beginning of the French Revolution

1790s	A revolt in Haiti against French rule, led by Toussaint L'Ouverture, marks the first independence movement in Latin America
19thC	Apex of the Industrial Revolution
1816	Bolivar defeats Spanish in Venezuela; independence confirmed in 1821
1829	The practice of *suttee* (widow burning) made illegal in India
1833	Slavery is abolished in British Empire
1848	"Year of Revolution" throughout Europe
1859	John Stuart Mill publishes *On Liberty*
1885	Conference in Berlin initiates the "Scramble for Africa"
1885	Indian National Congress is founded, beginning the campaign for home rule
1893	New Zealand becomes the first nation to fully establish a system of universal suffrage
Inter-war period	Extension of female vote; Great emergence of mass parties in Europe
1925	Mussolini becomes dictator in Italy
1927	Rise of Joseph Stalin in the Soviet Union
1933	Rise of Adolf Hitler in Germany
1944	First free presidential elections in Guatemala
1945	Defeat of the Axis Powers; Ushers in the process of democratization in Europe and Japan
1947	India and Pakistan gain independence
1948	The Marshal Plan helps rebuild war-torn Europe
1948	The UN approves the Universal Declaration of Human Rights, guaranteeing all people in all countries their basic rights
1951	Libya declares independence (beginning of post-war decolonization of Africa)
1956	Hungarian Revolution
1964	US Civil Rights Act bans racial discrimination in federal funding and employment
1968	The Prague Spring
1972	US Congress passes Equal Opportunity Act in response to growing women's movement
1976	Helsinki convention on human rights is adopted
1987	Mikhail Gorbachev introduces *glasnost*, or openness
1989	Fall of the Berlin Wall
1989	Popular pro-democracy protests take place in Beijing's Tiananmen Square
1991	The Soviet Union disintegrates as the Communist Party loses power; Democratic elections are held in Russia and throughout Eastern Europe
1990s	Use of the internet becomes widespread
1999	Nigeria and Indonesia elect democratic governments

from citizenship. Even for those who had the vote, elections were to be for 'representatives' who would govern in their stead. Such 'representation' was assumed quite indirect with the Member of Parliament retaining as much independence as was necessary for political stability and good order. This was a negative kind of consent – a freedom *from* arbitrary rule rather than a freedom *to* rule themselves.

In his work Macpherson traces this notion of freedom as it evolved out of older forms of obligation and hierarchy. He outlines 'possessive individualism' as follows:

1) The human essence is to use our capacities in search of our satisfactions.

2) Society is no longer a set of relations of feudal domination but a lot of free equal individuals related to each other through their possessions.

3) Political life is about the protection of these possessions – all capacities including life and liberty are considered 'possessions' rather than social rights and obligations. The rights to the use of property are thus fundamental.[3]

This notion of liberal democracy has less to do with methods of collective decision-making than with the protection of the individual from arbitrary interference. Those with more property obviously had more to lose and needed more protection from arbitrary interference. On the question of the arbitrary interference by those with more property against those with less, possessive individualism was silent. Thus liberalism was not inherently democratic, in fact it was hostile to the notion of full democracy.

Origins of weak democracy

This is the basis for the 'weak' notion of democracy that is still with us – a minimalist state should interfere as little as possible with the economic and political rights of individuals. The then-emerging market is seen as a more-or-less natural way of ordering human affairs.

But it must as much as possible be left to its own devices. It is not hard to see in this early 'possessive individualism' the kernel of contemporary arguments now fashionable with the New Right. Get government off the backs! Don't shackle wealth! Roll back government through a process of privatization, tax cuts, deregulation and so forth. Allow for the 'natural' operation of the market. Individual rights outweigh the collective democratic decisions of society. The former British Prime Minister Margaret Thatcher even went so far as to deny the very existence of society.

The emphasis of early liberalism (the democratic part came later) is on 'choice'. As Macpherson summarizes it: 'Instead of a society based on custom, and on status, and on authoritarian allocation of work and rewards, you have a society based on individual mobility, on contract and on impersonal market allocation of work and rewards in response to individual choices. Everyone was swept into the free market.'

In this market society the ideology of choice was extended to the political system and a limited number of voters: 'The electorate need not be a democratic one, and as a general rule was not; all that was needed was an electorate consisting of men of substance, so that the government would be responsive to their choices.'[4]

Another cultural strain of conservatism associated with the British conservative Edmund Burke and the French de Tocqueville projected a fear of the poor mob who threatened to topple the better sort of people. The denied right to vote then became a major focus of democratic struggles. Working class and feminist campaigners made the logical case that women and people without property were citizens too. These were long hard struggles of many dashed hopes and not a few dashed bodies. Many democratic activists devoted their lives to this fight.

It was not until the late 19th and early 20th century (several hundred years after the painful birth of liberal society in the English Revolution) that the battle to extend the democratic franchise to all adults was gradually achieved. But such struggles continued right up through the early 1960s' civil rights movement to enfranchise black people in the southern US and indeed to this day as different groups (immigrants, poor people, former prisoners, various minority groups) are excluded from voting. But despite the extension of the right to vote, the system of weak democracy still privileged those with enough wealth to shape and influence 'democratic outcomes'.

A strong democracy

From the earliest days of democratic thinking and development there emerges a struggle between a *weak* notion of democracy and a *stronger* version. It has continued to this day. Early proponents of the strong popular democracy were firebrands such as Thomas Paine, and radical theorists such as Jean-Jacques Rousseau. The French republican movement and advocates of early working-class politics such as the English Chartists and radical artisan movements across Europe continued to push the limits of market/property democracy. When the suffragist movement and various civil rights movements picked up the torch, they were advocating not merely the vote in national elections but also the extension of democratic equality into the family and the economy.

The propertied and conservative establishment in turn pushed back and tried to reduce democratic space. In shifting historical and geographic contexts this struggle continues. The notion of a strong democracy was propelled forward by the popular democratic impulse and the constant threat of democratic outbreaks from below. It found its intellectual reflection in a diversity of radical democratic ideas. On the other side there is a constant struggle to rein in democratic expectations and possibilities. Those with power and privilege see this as essential to maintain their rights in the market and their ability to manage the state.

Macpherson believes that the original theory of property-based democracy reflected the real economic conditions of a then-emerging capitalism. The notion of equality based on a 'republic of small-holders' (farmers, artisans, small business people) had some reality several centuries ago. But the theory has not kept up with the reality. The modern economy dominated by a couple of thousand transnational corporations and banks is a virtual economic dictatorship of global proportions. The response of the dominant stream of theory has been to abandon the idea that inequality of property had any political relevance. The right to vote and to protection of the laws was extended to all whatever their economic power. Thus the theory of liberal democracy was adjusted to defend the legitimacy of the extraordinary inequality of wealth and privilege that we see today.

Ratifying weak democracy

Most conventional political science has adopted the property-blind theory of liberal democracy as the one and only theory of democracy. Theorists devise prescriptions for weak democracy and the empirical attend to the mechanics of how systems in richer countries generally work and how poorer countries can bring their systems into line. They by-and-large eschew judgements about how democratic it actually is. So critical political philosophy and theory are displaced by detailed descriptions of how interest group competition works or comparing various constitutional arrangements.

Modern political and social science has clearly inherited the distrust of ordinary people and their capacities to participate in their own self-government. Most political scientists stress questions of political management and the comparative effectiveness of various élite systems of government. Participation (except passively during elections) is not to be encouraged.

Strong democracy: the urban crucible

'Who do you call when your toilet backs up?' This old political adage is a way of pointing out which level of government is most important to most people. Who do you depend on for physical security? Public health? Housing standards? Recreational facilities? Cultural amenities? Survival income when there is no other? It is usually the city or town council or whatever local authority exists. Granted many still do not have a toilet to back up (to say nothing of income). But the point remains valid that whether it is a village in rural India, a shantytown on the edge of São Paulo or an industrial suburb of Marseilles it is the local which is often crucial. As another old political sage put it 'all democracy is local'.

Sounds good in principle but it seems to be losing out in practice. Almost everywhere centralizing nation-states are sucking power away from the local. A market-oriented agenda of cutbacks, privatization and reorganization and 'economic rationalization' of local government is taking its toll. Municipal government is being reduced to a powerless 'service delivery' unit. A democratic deficit is being built up at the local level – with higher levels of government limiting the means to provide services while increasing the number of services to be provided.

In Toronto, Canada's largest city, the Conservative provincial government has redrawn municipal boundaries creating a city that no longer recognizes itself. Local self-governing municipalities were merged into a remote supercity. The number of local representatives elected has been dramatically cut. Torontonians resisted this move, voting some 70 per cent in a referendum to reject it. The Provincial government simply ignored the results and reshaped the city according to its cost-cutting whims. Without any legal constitutional status local democracy was at the mercy of central authority. And Toronto is not alone. The centralization of power away from the local and towards the regional is most visible amongst the world's burgeoning super-cities. Over the past quarter-decade these kinds of 'rationalization' of local government have hit everywhere from London to New York. Budgets have been slashed, powers reduced, mayoralties removed and then brought back. The ability to raise revenue severely restricted. With the municipal government at the sharp end of a number of crucial issues from homelessness and poverty to public transport and environmental deterioration – the loss has been not only to local democracy but to the quality of urban life.

But the centralizers have not had it all their own way. In Toronto, Citizens for Local Democracy has been waging a lively fight to revitalize grassroots power. They now form a network with a number of other organizations such as the Bread Not Circuses Coalition (resisting the city's Olympic bid), the Toronto Environmental Alliance and other activist groups working around homelessness, transit, tenants' rights, and a plethora of other issues that shape the quality of urban life. Together they put forward an alternate vision of what the city might be like if it controlled its own fate. You can find similar struggles going on in nearly ever major urban area. Cities across the globe have become points of resistance to the centralizing ambitions of the national political class. Back in the 1980s places like Bologna in Italy and Kyoto in Japan were models of cities whose approach to a balanced development involved a significant degree of popular empowerment rather than simply turning things over to the real estate lobby. More recently cities such as London (which elected independent mayoralty candidate Ken Livingstone), Mexico City (where the opposition PRD party holds power) and now Paris have taken up the fight to assert their own agendas and priorities in the face of a national state concerned more with cost-cutting and privatization than with providing the public goods necessary for a decent quality of urban life.

Cities and towns are often exciting sites of democratic experimentation. In the center of Copenhagen the alternative community of Christiania's use of self-government through direct popular participation is one example. Other towns like the Japanese seaport of Maki have used local referenda to frustrate the plans of the powerful National Nuclear Agency. If this is true in highly centralized Japan one can imagine the potential in societies like Thailand or Catalonia in Spain where local resistance to central power is the main currency of politics.

So with the majority of the world's population moving into cities it is heartening to see a growing municipal countertrend of resistance and experimentation in the face of a power-hungry national political class. This is particularly true as the nation-state mortgages local democratic rights (especially over economic issues) to the heavy hand of trade liberalization agreements administered by the World Trade Organization. Of course democratic forms will vary from smallish towns in the industrial North to the poor communities that surround Lagos in Nigeria and Peru's Lima. But all local forms have greater potential to be animated by the original democratic ideal that it is up to people themselves to decide. After all, it was in the urban crucible of ancient Athens, the Italian city-states, philosopher Jean-Jacques Rousseau's Geneva and the 1871 Paris Commune that many of our received notions of a strong democracy were forged. ■

Stability and the equilibrium of the system are held as higher values than participation and popular empowerment. The tilt is clearly towards a weak democracy.

This reflected the major intellectual currents that had gained predominance by the early 20th century. Sociologists like the German Max Weber focused on bureaucracy as the key to understanding the working of modern management systems. Others like the Swiss Michels and the Italians Mosca and Pareto formed a school of classic élite theorists and put forward an almost 'iron law of oligarchy'. This postulated (or rather insisted) that democracy was undermined by the inevitable rise of an élite in any complex organization whether a modern political party or a government. Pessimism about democratic possibilities became the norm. As the political economist Joseph Schrumpter famously concluded: 'Voters must understand that once they have elected an individual, political action is his [sic] business and not theirs. This means that they must refrain from instructing him about what he is to do.'[5]

The power of the people was plainly off the agenda. Political thinkers like Walter Lippmann in the US became much more concerned with the politics of mass persuasion (manipulation) than with the niceties of democratic rule. Perhaps the classic modern statement in favor of weak democracy is captured by the British Tory Prime Minister Winston Churchill when he proclaimed that 'democracy is the worst form of government except all those other forms that have been tried from time to time'. Faint praise indeed. A recent revealing if somewhat crude statement of the weak democracy position concluded *The Trouble with Democracy*, a lengthy tome by William D Gairdner. He believes we need to 'reclaim and revivify democracy with true classic liberalism and once again restore a rule of formal, as distinct from substantive, equality... defend the social and moral hierarchy, and the inequalities this produces, as natural to, and a mark of all free and spontaneous societies...'[6] In other words because inequality is written into human nature democracy can in no way be allowed to threaten accumulated wealth and power even if that wealth and power appear to violate democratic principles.

The Left abandons democracy

The main current of opposition to élitist theories of democracy came from the socialist Left. But the socialists, particularly those of the orthodox Marxist persuasion, have fumbled the democratic ball. They originally focused on overturning the dictatorship in the market and thus replacing Macpherson's 'possessive individualism' with a more broad-based citizenship. In the 19th and early 20th century no-one questioned that the Left stood for a broader more inclusive democracy – although many questioned whether this was possible or desirable. But the Left too abandoned democratic theory. As orthodox Marxism gained ascendancy on the Left it brought with it the assumption that once the market inequalities that undermined democracy were overcome, the self-rule of the workers would automatically emerge. Eventually the state and politics with it would 'wither' away and be replaced by a very technocratic-sounding 'administration of things' to use Marx's compatriot Friedrich Engels' phrase.

There was no need to work out the details of how this self-rule would operate and socialists took little interest in any theory of popular sovereignty that would act as a guarantee for a broader democracy. Indeed any such attempts were denounced as utopian. In hindsight these flaws proved fatal. With the first Soviet leader Lenin's autocratic adaptation of Marxism into a one-party rule 'dictatorship of the proletariat' ideas of workers' self-government receded into the far distant future.

Under Lenin's successor Stalin and later leaders the Soviet Union ossified into an autocratic state structure with an unresponsive and increasingly inefficient commandist economy. This police state approach to socialism and economic development gave away the Left's best argument. The natural advocates of a strong democracy had abandoned the field. Now the champions of the weak version of market-based democracy could point their fingers in horror at Soviet dictatorship and claim the exclusive democratic franchise. They became the only democratic game in town.

So both sides of the political spectrum are caught trying to reconcile (or denying the need to reconcile) the democratic power of the people with two fundamentally undemocratic structures – the market and the state. In the process democratic possibilities have atrophied and political thinking about democracy has stagnated. The revival of critical thinking that was sparked by the rise of the 1960s' New Left started to break this down. Some thinkers such as Herbert Marcuse and European Marxists like André Gorz and Henri Lefebrve sought a human agency to break the deadlock of weak democracy. Others in the South such as Franz Fanon and Amilcar Cabral sought ways of uprooting the colonial legacy of autocracy. But their emphasis was on liberation and not how a radical democracy might actually work.

Outbreaks of democracy

The end of the Cold War has created fertile ground for rethinking the fate of democratic ideals. There is now a rekindling of interest in democratic theory and practice that goes beyond the stalemate of state socialism and market-based weak democracy. It has been the consistent pressure of a democratic impulse from below and the continuous 'democratic outbreaks' that it stimulates which continue to keep democratic practice and ideals on the political agenda.

In a thoughtful essay the political scientist Ricardo Blaug describes the nature of contemporary democratic outbreaks and how they differ from the various versions of institutionalized democracy.[7] He stresses the episodic nature of these outbreaks and the way they transform passive spectators and consumers of politics to active agents creating informal networks and other forms of democratic action. In moments of political excitement people 'fly to the assemblies' in Rousseau's memorable phrase. Blaug concludes that 'democracy as a way of life has always been highly opportunistic'. It mushrooms into the political space vacated by the loss of order. Crisis, systemic breakdown, incompetent leadership all favor its spread. Examples of democratic outbreaks, some on a massive scale, are common in the history of religious struggles, agricultural uprisings, labor movements and secessionist rebellions. There is an unexpected and dramatic nature of such challenges. Blaug explains: 'Trained perhaps by generations of sovereigns and clerics we now concentrate our attention exclusively on political and cultural élites, and so cannot see the political activity which at last expresses itself in an outbreak of democracy.'[7]

Blaug identifies movements throughout the last century; everything from the spontaneous Danish resistance to the Nazis (yellow stars decorated the coats of tens of thousands of Danes in solidarity with the country's Jews) to the outbreaks of opposition to the Vietnam War, the formation of *Solidarity* in Poland and the revolt in Paris in 1968. Such revolts are sometimes local, provoked by an environmental outrage (an oil spill, nuclear power accident, or other toxic mishap) or by a particularly abusive act on the part of our political and economic managers. Outbreaks can redefine the political landscape as did the revolutions of 1848 which swept Europe that put absolutistic monarchy on notice. Such outbursts are almost inherently critical of weak democracy and push towards a more robust participatory form of democratic life.

These outbreaks can last hours or years but they provide the constant threat of popular agitation from below – a threat that haunts the political class. They occur, perhaps most profoundly and dangerously, in situations where the denial of democracy is blatant. We can see them at work all over the global South: the *force populaire* in Haiti risked the Ton Ton Macoutes death squads in the streets of Port-au-Prince... the East Timorese in their decades-long resistance to the Indonesian jackboot... the growing challenge to the theocratic authority of Iran's mullahs... the Chechens in their seemingly hopeless bravery in the face of Moscow's tanks... the Burmese in their intransigent opposition to military rule. In such places autocrats can be overthrown (or else would-be democrats slaughtered) and a situation of democratic possibility

Strong democracy: Korea's social movements

'We have no place to go from here.' These words are spoken by Nam Sang-wa, deputy-chairperson of the tenants' committee in Pynchong-dong, part of the bigger Bongchun-dong area of southeast Seoul. A dozen or so tenants are gathered in a living room in one of the houses that has so far escaped the wrecker's ball. Kids run in and out of the room, sitting on their parents' laps until they get restless from too much grown-up talk. And talk there is a-plenty. It swirls around them as they pass the verbal baton from one to the other to explain how the mechanics of property speculation affect poor people.

These are country people who have moved to Seoul in the last few years. On the hillside areas of greater Bongchun-dong poor people are making their last stand in a city rapidly being gobbled up by expensive high-rises. Too many people are chasing too little housing on increasingly expensive land. Absentee house-owners in Pynchong-dong sold out to a development company that, with government approval, has hired a demolition company to destroy their community. Already 75 per cent of the people have been forced out.

But some 134 households are determined to stay. They hold rallies – and drum festivals like the one that happened the previous evening. The demolition company, for its part, turns out the street lights and sets small fires. One of the tenants points to a house 100 meters down the road where some heavy-looking, tattooed guys are hanging out. He says they are members of street gangs the company has hired to harass people as they move up and down the hill.

The Pynchong-dong struggle is no isolated one. The tenants estimate can last for weeks or even years before some hardening of possibility into more-or-less 'representative' structures takes place.

These exciting times of political ferment – the Paris Commune in the 1870s, the People's Revolutions of Eastern Europe in 1989, Portugal after the overthrow of Fascism, the Tiananmen Square Movement in Bejing, Barcelona during the Spanish Civil War – were grand outbreaks and are in some sense the real stuff of democracy. They are at once messy, stimulating, full of citizen engagement and hope. Some have grand historic sweep and shift structures and memories inalterably. But they also occur on a less dramatic level around a thousand causes and grievances – citizens

that there are five major redevelopment zones in Seoul and some 500 different struggles to resist forced removal. Such 'quiet heroisms' have seen the democratic movement in South Korea through some pretty rough times. Korean social movements are highly organized affairs. They have local chapters and national offices, alliances and coalitions, executives and minutes. Files are neatly stacked, membership payments charted on walls. The residents of Pynchong-dong are connected to the Roomers' Association which is part of the Association of Urban Poor. This has some 80,000 members and is fighting for the rights of tenants, for decent daycare, and for street vendors who strive to create a life in the cracks of the Korean economy. These vendors add dynamism to Seoul's streets – whether they are selling huge juicy pears or setting up portable bars where one can sit and wash down a variety of seafood snacks. But they have become the latest target of the state's obsession with control from above. Restrictive zoning laws are being used to sweep them away.

Seoul's urban movements fight for the democratic space that will allow citizenship to flourish even in the most unlikely nooks and crannies of urban life. Implicit (and sometimes explicit) in their struggles is the notion of a strong democracy that moves beyond the ballot box. A democracy based on the notion that people have a right to control their own communities and protect their own ways of making a living. These urban struggles are connected to a tradition of militant defense by both workers and farmers of their rights. This has made Korea the site of some of the most combative struggles from below against the ravages of corporate globalization and for a strong democracy. ∎

who resist the weakening of local government authority by the national state… people who won't tolerate
the closing of the neighborhood school or the pushing through of a large highway… people who rally to
the defense of a besieged park or to halt the abuse of
a local ecosystem due to dumping of toxic wastes or
indiscriminate industrial logging.

These democratic outbreaks are the raw material of
a transformation of either autocracy or weak democracy into something deeper and more profound. In a
situation of a stronger democracy with channels of
popular pressure such initiatives have more of a
chance of success. A weak democracy tilts the odds in
favor of the managers of the system and their ability to
re-establish order and reassert market forces. So it is
not surprising that ideas for and experiments in a
strong democracy will flourish in such times.

But it is the democratic impulse – people's
unquenchable notion that in a democracy they
should get to decide – that is always the wild card. It
is never obvious when this sense will be violated and
the political apple cart will be overturned or at least
be made to teeter precariously. The Prime Minister of
Japan surely must have been surprised at the public
outrage simply because he didn't let the news of a
Japanese fishing boat sunk by a US nuclear sub upset
his round of golf. Whoever would have thought this
would result in the end of his political career? Or how
about the Canadian Government decision to provide
millions in financial aid to professional hockey teams
so that they could meet the salary demands of the
local ice gladiators. No reason to think that this corporate give-away, like so many others, would not be
accepted. Surely there would be the usual shrugs of
resignation. But after three days of popular outrage
the Government was forced into an embarrassing
climbdown.

Several years earlier, the recalcitrant Canadian public had rejected a top-down proposal (put to them in

referendum) to renew the Constitution, even though almost the entire political class was unified behind it. On occasion this kind of popular reaction can sweep across entire continents – as the revulsion with genetically-modified foods swept across Europe to the dismay of Monsanto et al. But questions still hang in the air – are these outbreaks by their very nature episodic? Can we find a way to build on them, to learn from them in order to deepen democracy?

The governability crisis

Some years ago orthodox political science started to worry about 'the governability of democracy' – the concept comes from the influential Harvard intellectual Samuel Huntington (also an advisor to Richard Nixon on the Vietnam War). Huntington's research (funded by the élite Trilateral Commission) advanced the notion that the system of government was being 'overloaded' with unrealistic popular demands for economic security and political input. In other words, *too much* democracy. Ways needed to be devised to protect the political class, to insulate them from popular pressure. Otherwise how could they make those tough unpopular decisions that were necessary to maintain stability and prosperity?

This was accomplished in a number of key areas. Some decisions, particularly those to do with economic policy, were either left to market forces to negotiate or put in the hands of powerful multilateral agencies like the World Trade Organization or the International Monetary Fund. In both cases they were safely beyond the reach of democratic pressure. A regime of privatization and cutbacks is being deployed to convince a 'spoilt' population of the notion that they are entitled to any but the most shoddy of public goods. Anything better will have to be purchased from the lucrative private sector by those who can afford it.

An elaborate national security state has gradually

taken shape, to 'police' democracy and protect politicians both personally and politically. So now when social movements seek to expand democratic space, they can be closely monitored and curtailed if they seek to use the 'illegitimate' means of street politics to advance their cause. A kind of constant low-intensity war, that pays little attention to democratic niceties, is waged against dissidents in many places. Disinformation (sometimes dressed up as public relations) is used to discredit them and invalidate their concerns. The security services deploy a wide range of snooping technologies that contribute to an elaborate national-security state with an inbuilt bias against those advocating change. The 'policing' approach is also extended to parts of the population considered either troublesome or not socially productive. Welfare provision is tied to policing the poor and forcing them into the lowest paid sectors of the labor market through benefit cuts and workfare schemes. Prison populations are on the rise as the behavior of various ethnic minorities, immigrant groups and youth are criminalized through the use of repressive drug laws. This combination of economic discipline and repressive policing is the current formula for sustaining weak democracy.

Reasserting democracy

But unease with this type of weak democracy is growing and not just at the grassroots. Major financiers such as George Soros, media czars like Ted Turner and other global luminaries, who meet every year at the famous (now besieged with demonstrators) Swiss resort town of Davos for the World Economic Forum, are starting to express concern that the present weak democracy approach – with its attendant inequalities of wealth and power – is causing a crisis of legitimacy for the system as a whole. Political thinkers such as the classic pluralist Robert Dahl, the dean of studies of democracy, now holds that the very pluralism that he once championed is being endangered by the power of corporate money swamping the political system.[8]

Dahl thinks that while market capitalism may initially help in the democratization of some poor countries it eventually rebounds to undermine that democracy: 'When authoritarian governments in less modernized countries undertake to develop a dynamic market economy, they are likely to sow the seeds of their own ultimate destruction. But once society and politics are transformed by market-capitalism and democratic institutions are in place, the outlook fundamentally changes. Now the inequalities in resources that market capitalism churns out produce serious political inequalities amongst citizens.'[9]

Dahl now believes that it is essential to re-organize the economy on democratic principles. Others such as the British political thinker David Held are proposing policies to extend democracy beyond the nation-state into the international domain to bring democratic pressure to bear on the forces and agencies of globalization previously beyond the reach of popular assemblies and elected officials.[10] From the grassroots, the anti-globalization movement is developing a challenge based on the idea of globalization from below to reassert democratic values. Other thinkers and democratic activists have put forward a range of proposals to strengthen democracy in the face of its obvious hijacking by the political class. So the tussle between a weak and a strong democracy is not about to disappear. It is being recast in contemporary terms, around issues of globalization and economic equality, and more democratic outbursts are just over the horizon. There are many positive signs that the stagnation in democratic political thought is coming to an end. The concern with 'liberation' that accompanied the 1960s' outbreaks is now shifting to one that explores the ways in which the exercise of popular power can actually shape social decisions. The trick will be to be able to ride this ferment of movements and ideas and use it to effect a long-term transformation that institutionalizes a popular power that can underpin a strong democracy. The following chapters will explore the potential for this in a number of key areas.

1 *Radical Democracy*, Douglas Lummis, Cornell University Press, Ithaca 1976. **2** *Socialism, Democracy and Self-Management*, Michael Raptis, Allison and Busby; London 1980. **3** *Democratic Theory: Essays in Retrieval*, CB Macpherson, Clarendon Press, Oxford 1973. **4** *The Real World of Democracy*, CB Macpherson, Canadian Broadcasting Corporation, 1975. **5** *Democracy*, Anthony Arblaster, University of Minnesota Press, Minneapolis 1987. **6** *The Trouble with Democracy*, William Gairdner, Stoddard, Toronto 2001. **7** 'Outbreaks of Democracy', Ricardo Blaug, *Socialist Register 2000*, Merlin Press, London 2000. **8** *A Preface to Economic Democracy*, RA Dahl, Polity Press, Cambridge 1985. **9** *On Democracy*, Robert Dahl, Yale University Press 2000 New Haven. **10** *Democracy and the Global Order*, David Held, Polity Press, Cambridge 1985.

4 Democratizing the economy

> *'To discuss democracy without considering the economy in which that democracy is to function is an operation worthy of an ostrich.'*
> **Adam Przeworski, sociologist.**

The lack of democracy in economic life undermines democracy everywhere else. Those with economic power – today largely major transnational corporations and banks – have myriad ways to get what they want out of the democratic process. A prerequisite for a more robust democracy is a coherent strategy to level economic and thus political inequalities. This chapter looks at entrenched economic power and evaluates the different strategies for challenging it.

FOR MOST PEOPLE the 8-odd hours (or more in many cases) spent at work has more to do with dictatorship than with democracy. While some workplaces have grown more relaxed the majority still closely monitor your time and what you do with it. When you arrive. When you leave. How you perform your tasks. How long you take for lunch. How many times you go to the bathroom. Who you talk to on the phone. The demeanor you adopt for your employer. All are prescribed in some detail whether you work as a security guard in Berlin or in a fast-food franchise in Seoul, a *maquiladora* clothing factory in Central America or making circuit boards in Penang. This most basic experience of life, earning your livelihood, involves the surrender of both your time and your will to the direction of others. This is a major deficit in the building of democratic life. The experience of a managerial autocracy at work robs people of a sense of their own democratic agency. It contributes to a passive 'follow orders' mentality that sucks away the lifeblood of active citizenship.

It is just not realistic to expect active citizenship from people who have so little power to influence the rest of their lives. A lack of democratic engagement leads almost inevitably to a passive consumerist approach to democracy. This is reinforced by a political class that has grown adept at manipulating consumer preferences in the 'political marketplace'. This is done through a virtual industry that runs expensive campaigns and projects elaborately-crafted images of honesty, sincerity and strength on the part of politicians. It is much easier to manipulate unreflective and insecure consumers of politics than it is to negotiate with a self-consciously activist citizenry. Consumerism in politics fits naturally into the consumer-oriented culture of 21st-century capitalism. When your main decisions revolve around choice of different cola and cigarette brands it is not a big jump to reduce democratic engagement to a choice between Brand X politician and Brand Y politician. If however you are used to having an active say in your workplace and community this is unlikely to satisfy you.

Contested terrain

The history of the industrial workplace is also a history of struggle for who is in control. In the earliest days of industrialism factory owners worked hard to wrest control of production from artisans who had power through their skills and knowledge of the production process. With the rise of scientific management inspired by the industrial engineer Frederick Taylor, work was divided into a series of easily-timed repetitive tasks on an assembly line, the speed of which could be controlled by the factory manager. Ever since, workers and their organizations have been engaged in an ongoing struggle to bring some democracy to the workplace. This has often focused on the conditions of work – making sure that jobs are safe and done at a human pace with adequate breaks. These struggles that many trade unions have committed themselves to deal with more than money issues and move 'beyond the fringe benefits'. They have also concentrated on the length of time spent working. The struggle for the 8-hour day has now been replaced by a movement for the 30- or 32-hour week. The idea is that work should not dominate life in the way that it has through most of the history of industrial capitalism.

It is a natural progression for workers and their unions to start demanding a say over investment decisions and what is done with profits. Should these go to stock dividends and CEO (boss) bonuses or be plowed back into the business to strengthen it? The point-of-entry for this kind of democratic demand is most frequently the issue of the right of capital to dispose of 'surplus' workers by simply laying them off.

The workers' movement has always demanded a say over this. But it has not stopped there. European unions particularly have tried to influence not only *how* things are produced but *what* is produced. The trade union movement has long been on the record for its opposition to military hardware and more recently in favor of ecologically benign products – public transit rather than private cars. The Australian trade union movement has battled against uranium mining and for green bans of construction projects that lead to a deleterious quality of urban life. On the level of governmental action, labor has traditionally called for intervention to limit owner/manager sovereignty over the workplace and to give broader guidance to investment and production decisions. Such demands are in direct violation of the rights of property that are at the center of the strong market/weak democracy model. To be truly effective however they must pull workers into action as citizens beyond what can be bargained on the level of individual enterprises.

Strange bedfellows

Capitalism and democracy have from the beginning been uneasy bedfellows. Most definitions of democracy imply a certain level of equality. Many of the original democratic theorists, Jean-Jacques Rousseau and Thomas Jefferson for example, imagined democracy would be based on a republic of more-or-less equal smallholders where economic equality was not a major issue. They never had to conceive of how it might work in a society with a small minority of wealthy investors and employers and a vast class of non-owners and employees.

Unequal citizens have unequal resources (money, time, education, inclination) to bring into the arena of democratic decision-making. If Microsoft's Bill Gates is worth $51 billion (£36 billion) he can buy a lot of 'democracy'. In these circumstances democracy is

---

Strong democracy: many faces of workplace democracy

Experiments in workplace democracy in the industrial North vary from small community-owned bakeries and artisan shops to entire industrial enterprises taken over by their workers – often as an alternative to bankruptcy. In the poor countries of the non-Western world self-organized enterprises are often the only alternative in the absence of private investors willing to undertake the risks and low profitability involved. While such endeavors come and go, they together mark a persistent effort by people to control their own economic fate and provide the seeds of a future democratic economy. Here are just a few examples:

• In five dusty Mayan villages on the Yucatan Peninsula in southern Mexico it takes the form of the Chac Lol Cooperative. Chac Lol (which is Mayan for 'red flower') produces corn tortillas. It runs five *tortillerias* that provide hot food for villagers. The co-op also runs several stores, a livestock farm of sheep and goats and a shoemaking enterprise.

The highest authority in the co-op is the General Assembly where all members get to vote. The structure is modeled on the Mondragon Co-ops of the Basque region in Spain. The co-op provides a living wage for those who work there and the economic and political independence from the PRI party which until recently had ruled Mexico for decades. According to Ester, one of the *cooperativistas* of Chac Lol, the co-op is an instrument of liberation providing a way for them to be owners of their own means of production. It provides better worker conditions and a higher standard of living, particularly for women.

• In Japan older workers are starting to form worker-run companies

---

eroded. The best of democratic theory assumes that some basic equality is necessary if citizens are going to exercise a more-or-less equal weight in shaping the direction of political life. Capitalism on the other hand with its ethos of 'possessive individualism' values above all the right to acquire as much property and wealth as possible. This is considered a just reward for an individual who exercises skill, ingenuity and initiative. The wealth and property thus acquired can be passed onto the next generation who may or may not be skilful and ingenious. Under capitalism inheritance has gradually created a class of wealthy people who control the productive resources of society (factories, real estate, capital, access to raw materials and credit).

in the face of the collapse of Japan's lifetime employment system. Older workers who are laid off find it particularly difficult to find new jobs. One such company, The Building Service Engineering Group, is made up of 70 worker-members whose average age is 66 years. This worker co-op, made up of ex-electricians and boilermakers, provides a building maintenance service. Revenues in the year 2000 soared to $1.3 million (£880,000). Most older worker co-ops focus not on profits but on providing stable employment under flexible conditions geared to the special needs of older workers so that they may lead well-rounded lives.

• In 1956 the Mondragon network was founded in the Basque region of Spain by a Catholic priest Don Jose Maria Arizmendi. This was the start of what has become one of the most significant experiments in workplace democracy in the modern world. The original worker-owned and managed factory named ULGOR numbered 24 members and manufactured kerosene stoves. Today the Mondragon cooperatives include over 86 production cooperatives averaging several hundred employees each. It also includes 15 building cooperatives, several service cooperatives, seven agricultural cooperatives, a network of consumer cooperatives with 75,000 members and its own bank (Caja Laboral) with 132 branches. Mondragon has over the years come in for its share of criticism for its compromises with managerial efficiency and the realities of capitalist business competition. But while some of these criticisms may be valid, Mondragon remains one of the few large-scale efforts at cooperative industrial organization, and as such has many lessons to teach. ■

This inherited advantage is today largely what dictates the life chances of most of us. While there is the occasional well-publicized 'rags to riches' story, most people realize that they have a better chance of winning the lottery than rising into the economic élite by dint of their own effort. The willingness of people to accept such inequalities is mute evidence of a shoulder-shrugging acceptance of the power of wealth to shape supposedly democratic outcomes.

Capital's veto power

Those with inherited or any other kind of wealth are in a position of considerable advantage in being able to influence the 'democratic' direction of that society. This is done both directly and indirectly. The health of the economy (and the well-being of everyone) depends on the investment decisions of the people who control capital and wealth in modern times through powerful transnational corporations. They want 'a good business climate' if they are going to continue to invest. This usually means a profitable return on what is invested, a competitive labor market, political stability, freedom from expensive regulations (perhaps around work safety or environmental controls), and taxation levels which do not discourage investors from 'risking' their money. Where a 'good business climate' does not exist investors are likely to 'strike' which could bring on a recession or even contribute to a depression. When the socialist government of François Mitterrand was elected in France in the early 1980s with promises of egalitarian reform, investment dropped right off. It went from the annual 4.4 per cent rate France had experienced from 1965 to 1980 to -1.21 per cent in the first three years of the socialist government.[1]

Other investor strategies may involve transferring their investments from less to more profitable sectors of the economy (say from steel to computers) or to transfer their investments to another part of the globe entirely to take advantage of a better business climate or 'lower wage jurisdiction' in say Bangladesh or the free trade zones of Mexico. It is obviously easier for some businesses (say textiles or electronics assembly) to take advantage by shifting to a more favorable investment regime than it is for others. Levi Strauss, the original manufacturer of blue jeans, has for example laid off almost 30,000 largely unionized workers in the process of shifting its garment factories to the low wage South.[2]

Occasionally an investor strike is not just an economic reflex but an overt political act as in Chile in the early 1970s when the international and Chilean business communities conspired to create conditions of political instability, laying the groundwork for the overthrow of the democratic government of Salvador Allende by a military dictatorship. Such overtly political 'investment strikes' are rare and usually unnecessary as most politicians are compliant and understand the rules of the game. More frequent are investment strikes that affect just one sector of an economy, for example the construction of rental housing, because of too strict rent controls; or investment in oil and gas exploration because of high royalties or taxes at the pump. The ability of major industries to run a kind of 'investors' auction' to see which jurisdiction (municipality, province, national state) comes up with the best package of pro-corporate policies severely restricts the right of communities to decide policy for themselves.

Debt squeeze

Another indirect way capital limits democratic possibilities is through the public debt held by nearly all nation-states and local governments as well. The political class is very nervous about offending those who hold the strings of debt (major private banks, the International Monetary Fund (IMF), The World Bank and so on). A bad report from the IMF or a revision of a credit rating by a big New York bond-rating agency like Salomon Brothers or Goldman Sachs can bring on a credit squeeze and endanger economic equilibrium. Debt in the South has reached crippling proportions. By 1997 its combined foreign debt had reached two trillion dollars. That is $400 per every man, woman and child which is more than many earn in a year.

Large creditors generally do not like policies which mean payments to them are taking second place to public spending on healthcare or education, no matter how necessary these are or how popular with the electorate. This is one of the major reasons behind the policies of 'structural adjustment' that have so devastated the South. It is highly contradictory for the North to pontificate about the lack of democracy in the South while insisting on policies that are by their nature undemocratic and must often be enforced by the use of police-state tactics. Witness the riots and protest movements born of the frustration with IMF-inspired cutbacks, price increases and currency devaluations. There is perhaps no clearer contemporary example of how democracy and the 'free' market are fundamentally incompatible. There may be other roadblocks to democracy (a predatory military, a corrupt state élite, entrenched religious authorities) but ending the arbitrary external imposition of economic policy is a vital, if not necessarily sufficient, step toward democratization.

Paying the piper

The other way the wealthy influence the direction of democratic decision-making is through the use of money to ensure favorable results. This direct consequence of 'some being more equal than others' is more visible and thus more controversial than the indirect veto (although perhaps not as effective) as many see it as a question of simply 'buying' democracy. Yet this is also quite complex and works itself out in a myriad of ways. Those with money can contribute to politicians and parties (usually but not always conservative ones) so they can run more visible and effective campaigns. More money means more ads on TV and everywhere else. More money means a more effective campaign machine, more highly-paid pollsters, more tele-canvassing, more focus groups, bigger, more lavish rallies, the best professional designers, consultants and spin doctors. The list is almost endless, and given that the last US election is estimated to have cost the candidates a billion dollars, it is growing longer all the time. The corrupting influence of money on campaigns is somewhat alleviated in those places with stricter spending controls and limits than the US but it still plays a large role almost everywhere. And as US political consultants spread their vision and their skills to 'export' markets, such controls are coming under increased pressure.

Then once politicians do get elected, those who can afford to pay well-connected lobbyists who understand how to influence the complex legislative process are 'more equal' than everyone else who just sits in front of the TV and wonders where all that new spending on health care or poor children or those tougher environmental regulations have disappeared to.

In most cases we are not talking anything as crude as direct bribery – although as organizations like Transparency International continue to show this remains a serious problem in the sphere of the former Soviet Union and much of the non-industrial South. In China it is estimated that as much as 8 per cent of the Gross National Product goes from foreign capitalists to the families of the ruling Party bureaucracy in order to set up and operate in the newly liberalized economy. China is of course not a democracy but a similar process of buying officials and politicians is widely held to go on in India over the rewarding of defense contracts. Bribes in the democracies of the industrial world have more to do with job opportunities once you leave office.

But usually the process is an altogether more subtle

one. It is a question of showing legislators sensible and realistic compromises that do not step on corporate toes. Watering down this piece of legislation. Pushing for voluntary compliance rather than direct enforcement of work or consumer safety and environmental standards. Pointing out how 'out of step' regulation or other public intervention is compared with what is happening in other more market-friendly jurisdictions.

Shaping the debate

Another corporate 'more equal' effect on the democratic agenda is achieved by using their resources to shape public debates. Hundreds of millions of dollars are spent every year to hire expensive public relations companies like Ogilvy Worldwide, Burson-Marsteller, and Hill and Knowlton who are expert at finding the best way to put out the corporate message. The income growth of the PR industry was an astounding 263 per cent between 1978 and 1998.[3] Money is spent on advocacy ads to push for a decrease in capital gains taxes or to uphold the democratic right of tobacco companies to sell their products. Money can be used to cultivate journalists and other opinion makers. To 'greenwash' the behavior of oil and mining companies environmental education kits can be offered free of charge to cash-strapped educational institutions. Corporate names and logos pop up almost everywhere from product placement in the movies or on TV, corporate dedications that appear on sports stadiums or your local public library. The ubiquitous Nike swoosh is the classic example. With the public realm squeezed of resources don't be surprised if you local library gets named after the McDonald's hamburger chain. The corporate message amplified by the liberal use of cash is by far the loudest to be heard in the democratic arena.

Welfare capitalism

The major effort to reconcile unbridled capitalism with democratic values has been through the evolution of an extensive regulatory and welfare state. The welfare state restored a modicum of balance between the demands of capital for profitable investment opportunities and the needs of everyone else. Starting in the Great Depression and picking up speed at the time of World War Two and after, this hybrid government attempted to ameliorate the worst inequalities of the system and prevent corporate abuse of the citizenry. Gradually a kind of consensus started to take shape that didn't much interfere with corporate domination of the economy but counterbalanced corporate power in the more general public interest. Such policies oversaw unprecedented growth based on the notion that government spending and national employment policies could counter or at least dampen the boom-and-bust business cycle. With the march to power of New Right in the 1980s this consensus came under heavy attack. A Keynesian program and the idea of government implementing a national economic strategy were replaced. An agenda of deregulation, cuts in social entitlements, and reduction of the public sector swept across almost all borders. Democratic attempts to counterbalance the inequities of the market went into free fall. With the intensification of globalization in the 1990s and accompanying draconian policies of market-oriented structural adjustment in the global South, inequities of wealth reached levels not seen since the days of robber baron capitalism in the late 1890s. It is perhaps not surprising that the period from the 1890s up until World War One can be identified as the first great wave of corporate-led globalization. The accompanying inequities of power (then and now) have succeeded in stunting the democratic promise.

Through myriad ways, both direct and indirect, the rampant inequality in both economy and society is poisoning whatever democracy we have left. The underpinnings of a formal political democracy are constantly undermined by inequality. Its increase over the last couple of decades in the context of a global economic life dominated by a couple of hundred major transnational corporations and banks bodes poorly for our democratic future. These corporations are constantly gobbling each other up (Chemical Bank and Chase Manhattan, Bank of America and Security Pacific) creating fewer and fewer players at the top. They now dominate some two-thirds of global trade. In straight economic terms the major corporate players outweigh an increasingly large number of sovereign states.

The perceptive social critic Christopher Lasch points out the near impossibility of limiting the distorting impact of wealth on democratic outcomes. He believes that 'the difficulty of limiting the influence of wealth suggests that wealth itself needs to be limited. When money talks everyone else is condemned to listen. For that reason a democratic society cannot allow unlimited accumulation.'[4] It is quickly becoming a question of either democratizing the economy or having a despotic economy sweep away the last vestiges of meaningful political democracy. While no one is about to take away your right to vote, whether or not you exercise that right will matter less and less.

The ideological sleight of hand used to reconcile market domination with political democracy is the notion that connects unimpeded market activity with an economic freedom. This is then taken to be the basis of political freedom. This was indeed a powerful argument when it juxtaposed itself to the economic inefficiencies and shortages of the despotic state socialism of the Soviet sphere. It even had some resonance for critics of corrupt state bureaucracies in the global South and those who decry the arbitrary nature of welfare state bureaucracies in the North. But today most of this is history: even the authoritarian socialism of China and Vietnam is adapting itself to the market as the main tool for organizing economic life. They have been very successful in doing this, particularly China which has experienced phenomenal economic growth, while maintaining the despotic rule of the Party. This is proof (if any were still needed after the sordid history of corporate partnerships with the various military dictatorships of the South) that the economic freedom of the market is perfectly compatible with a lack of any basic democratic rights in the political sphere. This severely undermines the case of the 'free market' liberal economic and political analysis. Today's icons of this 17th-century truth, the neoliberal economic philosophers Frederich Van Hayek and Milton Friedman and the whole edifice of well-funded New Right thinking they inspire, are hard-pressed to explain these new forms of market despotism. The notion that political and market freedom necessarily go hand-in-hand is being done violence by the facts.

Economic freedom or economic democracy

It is a major misnomer to refer to 20th-century global capitalism as an example of economic freedom at all. This is a global economy dominated by a few hundred major transnational corporations and banks who control the fates of not only the tens of thousands who work for them but also most of the world's nation-states who must compete for their favors. Most are dwarfed and thus intimidated by their economic might. Economic freedom in production belongs to those with access to capital and technology. Economic freedom in consumption belongs to a minority of the world's consumers who can afford access to the cornucopia of brand name products that are supposed to make up the good life. Even they must pay the price of the insecurity of living under a mountain of consumer debt. This liberal notion of economic freedom is a highly individual one whose only social dimension lies in the increasingly dim hope that the invisible hand of the market will harness private vice to create some distant overall public good. This is proving less and less defensible as social inequalities reach obscene proportions, the global ecosystem creaks under the weight of un-directed market-led growth and the democratic promise is turned into a hollow shell.

Economic freedom and economic democracy are not the same thing. Economic democracy implies not a series of unimpeded individual and corporate rights but a collective process for controlling economic life. There is a vast amount of experience and theory involved in trying to do this. And while movements to democratize economic life have achieved only partial and limited results this is largely due to an inhospitable context and the strength and determination of the foes of economic democracy – the corporate powerholders who dominate the world economy.

Debates between partisans of economic democracy tend to revolve around the role of the market. The core issue has to do with whether the market can be made to serve a democratized economy or whether it will inevitably undermine it.

It is possible to identify several tendencies in the ongoing struggle for an economic democracy:

State socialism
This was once the main alternative to market capitalism. Classic Marxist theory modified by Lenin held that central planning under a scientific élite working through the 'dictatorship of the proletariat' would reorder the economy in the interests of the broader society. This was the classic Communist economy seen throughout eastern Europe, the former USSR and Asian communism. Although this highly centralized planning was helpful in the first phases of industrialization (at significant cost to both human and workers' rights), it quickly ran out of steam and major economic problems started to emerge. Shortages, corruption, gross inefficiencies and waste, and a chronically poor environmental record plagued state socialism. There was no effective feedback mechanism from below to indicate the economic wishes of society.

Neither did its promise to democratize the economy amount to much as the bureaucrats in charge of production and planning ossified into a more-or-less permanent stratum. There was no real attempt to replace even the minimal feedback mechanisms of the market with more democratic forms that could articulate the desires of producers and consumers.

The regulatory state
In classic pluralist political theory this is the solution put forward to 'counter-balance' the weight of those who dominate the market. The idea is that the interests of society (to provide public goods such as health and transportation, protect consumers, workers and the environment, legislate inequalities, etc) would be enforced by government. This state would be subject to influence by the whole range of opinion (environmentalists, unions, consumer groups) who would ensure an adequate level of regulation in order that market forces are channeled to meet a general public interest. But as we have seen in practice this is a contest of unequals with the combined weight of the corporations with all their resources smothering alternative views and possibilities. Even the classic theorists of pluralism such as Robert Dahl have come to recognize that these power inequalities threaten the foundations of democratic contestation. The regulatory state has also adopted a very hierarchical top-down style which has alienated public opinion. There has been little consistent effort to democratize government and involve an active citizenry in helping to police inequitable and unecological market outcomes. To make matters worse this popular hostility to an arbitrary and bureaucratic state has been seized on and amplified by conservative politicians. The resulting neo-liberal offensive has been used to help roll back government, increasing inequalities and putting the environment and public health in jeopardy.

Market socialism

This theory is a modification of socialist doctrine brought about by left-wing economists such as Oskar Lange, W Brus and Alec Nove reacting to the failures of state socialism's command economy. The case is most persuasively put forward in Nove's 1983 study *The Economics of Feasible Socialism.*[5] This basic adaptation of socialist theory holds that while most productive property (factories, natural resources, access to credit) should be either socialized or held cooperatively, the market remains the best way to decide things like prices, the flow of labor and most decisions to invest. Their idea is to combine the efficiency of the market with the democratization of productive units to ensure that no private monopolies can displace the public interest. Where investment decisions involve major externalities (effects on, say, the environment) a democratically accountable system of central planning would still have a role. Some sectors like health and education would be exempt from market-type criteria. The 'market socialists' envision a maximum of democratic consultation (they vary on the possibilities for workers' self-management) in factories and offices thus overcoming the passivity of wage labor and enhancing active citizenship. There would need to be a continuing role for a regulating state to lay the ground-rules of the economy, establishing broad agreement on incomes policy and taxes, and ensuring (in the absence of the corrupting influence of a corporate élite) that the market continue to serve the social goals.

Planning from below

Planning from below is a strategy for democratizing the economy more in line with the classic socialist vision. It foresees only a minor role for the market and puts the emphasis on a system of democratically-controlled co-ordination of economic life. There are many versions of this, from radical visions of a highly decentralized society that has abolished money to elaborately thought-out systems for running advanced industrial economies. Some, such as the famous advocate of decentralization, EF Schumacher and those he has influenced, see democratic control of investment and development at the local community level as the key.

The British political economist Pat Devine in his *Democracy and Economic Planning*[6] puts forth a model based on what he calls 'negotiated coordination'. He details a system that would combine decentralization of decisions with the development of new democratic bodies like 'interest sections' and 'accountable planning commissions' at all levels of the economy. There would be workers' self-government in all enterprises. Planning advocates like Devine believe that market socialism relies too much on competing self-interests and will impede the emergence of a truly self-governing society and an economy that is organized around the democratically-decided goals of human beings. Devine identifies the high-level of management and administration that are already part of modern economies as an inevitable departure from a 'pure market'. He feels that if these were properly democratized they could act as the basis of a 'negotiated coordination' of an economy planned from below. He places a heavy emphasis on the achievement of equality and equal influence to create the capabilities necessary for a truly self-governing society.

The socialized market
This proposal for democratizing economic life is closely associated with the UK economist Diane Elson.[7] She and other advocates of the 'socialized market' believe a strategy that bends market outcomes to social purposes will allow democratic intervention in a variety of ways that would ensure more popular control. Elson proposes a dramatic extension of common property rights over investment that would work

through a system of participatory regulation to enforce social and ecological criteria on all major investment decisions. She believes that the seeds for this already exist in a range of corporate accountability initiatives that deal with such matters as minority hiring, child labor, working conditions and environmental impacts. The 'socialized market' would include a basic income for all and reinforcing those markets (which Elson calls 'associative' and 'provisioning') would decentralize power and promote values of solidarity. Advocates of a socialized market believe that it is necessary to move beyond a sterile debate between 'market' and 'plan'. Elson concludes that 'my vision is not a "market" society but not a "bureaucratic" society either; it is a society in which democratically accountable state agencies structure markets so as to give a much greater chance for households and associations to flourish.'

The democratic economy debate

The debates among the different positions of how best to democratize the economy tend to revolve around the differing weights given to planning and the market. While the 'socialized market' position represented claims to transcend this debate – it does so only by looking at plan and market in different ways. It does not dispense with them. The key issue is whether or not market relations can be molded to reflect a broad range of interests or whether they inevitably serve those who are successful in achieving commanding monopolistic market power (as they do in a corporate-dominated economy). An auxiliary question has to do with whether market transactions will inevitably generate inequalities. And whether they can be made to take into account the use of natural resources and the impact of pollution.

Another issue revolves around whether the regulatory state can be made to reflect a consistent public interest, rather than unfairly reflecting the interests of those with market power as they do now. Advocates of 'democracy through planning' also have a number of serious issues to face. To what degree can planning of a highly complex economy be democratized? How can popular involvement and the technical expertise needed to run a modern economy be reconciled? How can a workforce and communities with little experience (or maybe even interest in) running an economy be given the confidence and motivation to do so? How can democratic institutions be developed to ensure a balance between the needs of consumers, producers and all the other interests (the environment, public health)? If the market is in danger of breeding inequalities, there is a danger that planning will degenerate into a top-down commandist approach. This would undermine popular participation and democratic possibilities.

These debates are fruitful and exciting. Their common starting point is that without a thorough-going democratization of economic life, even the present minimal level of political democracy we enjoy will be undermined. Democracy does not stand still. It is either extended or it retracts. It is clear that the present undemocratic organization of the economy inevitably undermines the equality needed to sustain a political democracy.

Nearly all advocates of economic democratization identify a role for workplace democracy as crucial. The dictatorship that most experience at work saps democratic self-confidence in the population. Some economic democracy advocates fear that with total self-management, workers would make the same narrow profit-seeking decisions as private corporations. They want to balance the power of self-managed economic units with that of consumers and others who could address the shortcomings of particular investment decisions. It is clear however that a much greater input from workers on investment and other production decisions, and self-governance of the rhythms and conditions of work (hours, shifts, holidays, pay, breaks, etc) are crucial for any democratic economy.

Disciplining democracy

Douglas Lummis in his excellent study *Radical Democracy* draws a parallel between the role that the military used to play in limiting democracy with that of the role of the contemporary economy. It was the Prussian Wilhelm Von Merchel who declared that 'the only remedy for democrats is soldiers'. And throughout the history of democratic struggle from Republican Rome to Pinochet's Chile, the bodies of democrats are piled very high indeed. But Lummis believes that the economy has now taken over the role of limiting democracy: 'daily life is the economy, the very control system... captured in the ominous expression "business as usual"... democracy cannot be satisfied with a politics defined as a leisure activity driven out of the center of life (the economy) into occasional bits and pieces of "surplus". The democratic project will not be completed until it has succeeded in democratizing work.'[8]

A democratic economy requires a high degree of decentralization as a way of empowering local people and communities to control their economic destiny. For some this means a high-level of self-reliance (even autarky). Others see it possible to combine decentralization with systems of equitable trade.

The various strategies for achieving economic democracy are not just pie-in-the-sky. They can be seen in the cooperative sector at work in most economies. In the attempts to build fair trade between Northern consumers and Southern producers. In workers' struggles for more say on the job. In the various attempts to decentralize and democratize state socialism. In the democratic challenge to market-based investment criteria by movements to control workers' pension funds or other forms of ethical and socially responsible investing. All these efforts have a partial slightly inadequate feeling to them. They are not by-and-large part of an overall strategy to democratize economic life. And such attempts often feel like 'one step forward, two steps back' given the inhospitable climate in which they must struggle to survive. But they don't disappear. They keep popping up in a rich variety of forms. They are proof of the desire and indeed need for people to control their economic destiny – not just as atomized consumers and entrepreneurs but in a social and collective sense.

The present situation in our limited democracy is one where the political class that manages the economy takes the advice and is beholden to the interests of those who have managed to accumulate significant market power. A real democracy would be one where the tasks and priorities of economic management were based on the advice and beholden to the interests of the broader society. Whatever the mixture of market, plan, socialized market, workers' self-management, decentralization, fair trade and ethical investment needed to achieve this must be worked out in practice and through creative experimentation. The exciting debate about what a democratic economy should look like can only stimulate this process. The fate of our current fragile and partial political democracy hangs in the balance. Only a thorough-going economic democracy will enable us to deepen and strengthen it.

Only in an economy beholden to the interests of the entire society can we hope to bring an end to what the French social theorist André Gorz calls the domination of economic reason. This kind of all-inclusive economic rationality expressed through the under-regulated market cancels out the possibility of an economics based on a thought-out human purpose. 'The market itself is not the goal of any of the actors that confront one and other there; it is the space that results from their confrontation just as "traffic" is the result of all those who are driving their cars at any particular moment and have... an average speed imposed upon them by all the other drivers, none of whom has actually chosen it.'[9] At the moment this economic rationality (a rationality lacking reason in Gorz's view) is creating a world of compulsory labor that produces too much, uses up too many resources, distributes its rewards unfairly and is endangering the global ecosystem upon which we depend to survive. Only a viable economic democracy has a chance of redirecting economics to serve some sane human purpose – where people control capital, rather than it controlling us.

1 *Democracy and Capitalism*, Samuel Bowles and Herbert Gintis, Basic Books, New York 1987. **2** *New Internationalist* No 322, p 11. **3** O'Dwyer's Directory of Public Relations Firms, New York 1978 and 1998. **4** *The Revolt of the Elites*, Christopher Lasch, Norton 1995. **5** *The Economics of Feasible Socialism*, Alec Nove, George Allen and Unwin, New York 1983. **6** *Democracy and Economic Planning*, Pat Devine, Polity Press, Oxford 1988. **7** 'Socializing Markets, not Market Socialism', Diane Elson, *Socialist Register 2000*, Merlin Press, London 2000. **8** *Radical Democracy*, Douglas Lummis, Cornell University Press, *Socialist Register 2000*, Ithaca 1996. **9** *Critique of Economic* Reason, André Gorz, Verso, London 1989.

5 Beyond the nation-state

'The democratic idea itself is perhaps best thought of as a utopian aspiration... we need such aspirations if we are to resist the notion, made plausible by the seeming inevitability of globalization, that democracy, self-determination and the common good are ideas whose time is past.'

Steven Newman in
Globalization and Democracy.

Globalization and the politics of influence practised by the major world powers is a constant limitation on popular sovereignty. It takes decisions out of the hands of elected officials or at least gives them the excuse not to act. This chapter evaluates the different efforts to move democracy beyond the nation-state – from structures of regional governance to the evolution of an international civil society and a cosmopolitan democracy.

DEMOCRACY IS USUALLY associated with the nation-state. The liberal-democratic model of a weak democracy based on possessive individualism emerged in the 17th and 18th centuries not long after the nation-states of Europe and North America were themselves consolidated. While democracy does have broader deeper meanings its association as a system of rule within the context of national sovereignty leaves the nation-state as the main site of democracy (or the lack of it) in most people's understanding. We speak of whether a state is democratic or not. Or whether it has a good or bad record on democratic rights.

But sovereignty has always been limited in the inter-national system of state relations that lie outside the control of even the most committed democrats. The difference between the United States or China and

Gabon or Trinidad when it comes to the exercise of their respective national sovereignties is large indeed. Their capacity for maneuver to meet the needs of their citizens varies dramatically. If there is conflict between them it is never really a contest of equals. If for example there is a clash between the interests of a US-based oil company and an indigenous community in a remote corner of Ecuador, the capacity of the Ecuadorian government to protect its citizens (assuming it even wants to) is limited by its overall relationship with the United States. The sordid history of gunboat diplomacy stretching across centuries – from Cortez in slaughtering the Aztecs in Mexico to US jets firing rockets into Iraq – is ample evidence that 'might makes right' is an enduring principle of international relations.

In ordinary times it is usually more subtle diplomatic and economic influences that are used by the more powerful to get the less powerful to accede to their wishes. The speedup of the pace of globalization and the rise of rules-based trade agreements enforced through the World Trade Organization and regional agreements like the proposed Free Trade Area of the Americas limit the sovereignty of nation-states, particularly on economic matters. In the last few decades there has been a 'downsizing' of the capacity of most nation-states to shape their own internal affairs, particularly in the realm of economics. The central thrust of globalization strips governments of their capacities to protect their own populations from the ravages of international competition. The economist Marjorie Cohen concludes that 'international trade agreements provide the impetus for the proliferation of minimalist states whose major function for the international regime will be to control their own people to ensure that they conform to the international trade rules.'[1] The globalization agenda has implicit in it a kind of 'downsized democracy' where democratic majorities can only protect the quality of their lives within the bounds set by a collection of corporate-inspired trade and investment rules. This has obvious implications for the kinds of democracy that are possible.

Overturning democracy

The kinds of policies that exist today in the industrial world (and significant parts of the South) came about through some kind of democratic process no matter how imperfect. Change in such policies would usually require a public debate and often some kind of legislative act by an elected assembly of some sort. Cohen, echoing the views of an increasing number of critics of economic globalization, points out that 'Now, economic and political policy can be challenged through

international trade law. These are laws that are inter-
preted and enforced by people on a plethora of
international panels who are not elected and who do
not have to respond to people, since individuals within a country have no access to them.'[2] In other words
many of the rules for ordering economic (and by
implication political) life are set outside the democratic reach of most citizens.

This may not matter too much for those who are
happy that the uncontrolled market is the best way to
organize economic life. But for groups seeking more
equality in everything from income distribution to
regional development it is a very effective way of
tying their hands. It also places significant obstacles
in the path of those who value environmental integrity or worker health and safety over the
profit-maximizing behavior on which the liberalization agenda is built.

The diminished power of the nation-state has
become a major source of concern for political
thinkers of all persuasions. For some it provides a welcome stability and a useful economic discipline on
wayward politicians. For others it is a major violation
of the democratic prerogatives of the citizenry from
Bangkok to Berlin. But this is not just a matter of
polite debate at learned conferences and in weighty
academic journals. It has a real impact on people's
lives and has provoked what may be the most profound democratic outbreak since the 1960s.

The anti-globalization movement

It started in the South and has spread rapidly to the
point where the architects of liberalization are now
being challenged at every turn. Perhaps the first clear
shot came back in October 1983 when half a million
Indian farmers staged a day-long rally in Bangalore to
protest at proposals for liberalizing agricultural production. Next it was the Zapatista revolt in Chiapas on
1st January 1994 which shook Mexico and brought

into question the newly-signed North American Free Trade Agreement (NAFTA). The Zapatistas called this treaty 'the death certificate of the indigenous people of Mexico'. The democratic outbreak against trade liberalization spread like wildfire. Hundreds of street demonstrations and protests, petitions and conferences, food riots and campaigns followed in rapid succession. Networks of activists from both North and South shared tactics and strategic perspectives. Soon the whole trade liberalization program had become highly controversial. Revolt spread from the South to the North culminating in massive demonstrations against the World Trade Organization in Seattle which resulted in a collapse of negotiations for a new global trade agreement. Now street demonstrations and counter-conferences have become the norm accompanying every major meeting that tries to advance the economic liberalization agenda. The common theme of this resistance is the belief that the liberalization agenda bypasses the democratic process. It disenfranchises citizens, taking away their democratic choices in order to conform to a regime of trade and investment rules designed to protect the prerogatives of transnational corporations. The environment, worker and minority rights, social and economic equality, balanced regional development, the provision of new public services and the position of the small farmer are all on the block as a consequence of this process.

Debate in the movement

A key debate amongst critics of this usurpation of democracy is over how best to deal with the globalization offensive. There are two positions emerging on the best way forward. One stresses the need for structures of democratic governance and an international civil society beyond the traditional nation-state. The other advocates the reassertion and possible enhancement of the traditional powers of the nation-state. It maintains that the nation-state is the proper site for democratic decisions to emerge. It holds that democratic arrangements are best organized and can only really work on a national basis. Advocates of this position generally feel that most multilateral institutions – everything from the International Monetary Fund to the United Nations or the International Court in the Hague – have an inbuilt tendency to be hijacked by powerful interests. *Fortune 500* transnational corporations and banks or superpowers such as the United States are just better equipped to play the international game. The evidence for this is clear enough. By and large the institutions of global economic management have been consistently committed to what has come to be known as 'the Washington Consensus.' This is a fundamental belief that market relations should guide economic decision-making and that government intervention should be as much as possible discouraged. Public sector investment, subsidies to keep food prices down or to prop up small farmers, an industrial strategy designed to overcome regional disparities, an increase in the minimum wage are all policies that fly in the face of the Washington Consensus. It matters little if they are wildly popular with the electorate. The substantial weight of the World Bank, the International Monetary Fund and the World Trade Organization will continue to be subtly (and not so subtly) brought to bear to discourage such policies.

The United Nations

And it is not just the economic sphere in which the exercise of naked power politics takes place. The United Nations which is supposed to rise above power politics and aspire to lofty international values has been plagued by superpower domination. The world's most powerful nations (the US, Russia, China, France and the UK) hold seats as permanent members of the Security Council (with a veto on all resolutions) of the

UN. As members of the Council they are able to exercise influence far beyond the weight of their respective populations. The global South on the other hand is held in relative powerlessness throughout the UN system. During the Cold War the US had a particularly disdainful attitude towards the UN, regarding it as a 'bastion of the Third World and a center of socialist bombast'.[3] US politicians could always win brownie points at home by attacking UN waste and the supposed anti-Americanism that held sway there.

With the end of the Cold War however the UN became useful for successive US administrations bent on policing actions in various trouble spots around the world. The criteria for intervention had more to do with US strategic interests than with the amount of genocide or the number of refugees. Bosnia and Rwanda were allowed to burn but Kuwait with all that oil was another matter entirely. The Gulf War was the first example of clothing a fairly blatant US-led military intervention in the cloak of UN multilateralism. The bombs started to fall before any UN resolution was passed. Not that official Washington goes out of its way to hide its cynical manipulation of the UN. According to John Bolton, an undersecretary in the State Department responsible for UN affairs at the time of the Gulf War: 'The success of the United Nations during the Gulf War was not because the United Nations had suddenly become successful. It was because the United States through President Bush demonstrated what international leadership, international coalition-building, international diplomacy is really all about... When the United States leads the United Nations will follow. When it suits our interests to do so, we will do so. When it does not suit our interests, we will not.'[4] Hard to be blunter than that.

Winner's justice
Even the international court of justice in the Hague stands accused (with some justice but also a lot of

hypocrisy by those trying to divert attention from their own crimes) of dispensing 'winner's justice' on the question of war crimes. It would never even consider whether those responsible for the decisions of aerial warfare no matter how high the 'collateral damage' (civilian death toll) should be charged. So those advocates of democratic reform that are suspicious of attempts to build a counterweight in international institutions to balance both the arbitrary nation-state and the power of corporate globalization have ample evidence to back up their beliefs. The UK political

International civil society

Greenpeace, born on the Pacific shores of British Columbia, now monitors and supports struggles for environmental integrity worldwide from its international headquarters in Amsterdam. The Pesticides Action Network, a worldwide coalition of groups and individuals, exposes the dangers to food and foodworkers from the Philippines to Peru. The International Lesbian and Gay Association headquartered in Brussels links 350 groups in 70 countries engaged in the fight for the rights of sexual minorities.

These days it is not only nation-states and organizations representing nation-states (all the UN-related agencies) that operate in the international arena. Of course for centuries business has also done so. Initially this was mostly merchant traders who would buy cheap and sell dear. Then it was finance capital. Gradually extractive industry and agribusiness became international. Manufacturing followed. Now transnational corporations dominate the global economy controlling nearly two-thirds of global trade.

Since World War Two however non-commercial organizations have started to spread their wings beyond their borders of origin. Representatives of Amnesty International in Pakistan write letters to stop capital punishment in the US, while US members rally in support of Pakistani political prisoners. International organizations of writers like PEN International struggle to maintain the democratic space necessary for creative expression wherever threatened. International trade union organizations combine with student activists to expose sweat shop labor practices of the brand-name (the labor behind the label) clothing manufacturers from Central America to Cambodia. It's the same story with nurses, journalists, metal workers, lawyers and countless other groups. They are all finding it increasingly necessary to have an effective voice on the international stage.

writer Timothy Brennan makes the case succinctly: 'We need to be very cautious in contemplating any cosmopolis that would short-circuit the existing nation-states in the name of the people: on that imaginary terrain too many powerful interests are already entrenched.' He believes that 'within a world system in which enormous disparities in national power persist, structures that give some chance to local or indigenous peoples to draw a boundary between what is theirs and what lies beyond, between what is open to the outside world and what is sheltered from it [are vital].'[5]

Development NGOs link together in 'international families' based on a rough similarity of approach – some fight for social justice and to end political poverty, others provide micro-credit or run foster parent schemes. Many feel the need to engage the major players of the global economy whether Nestlé's for marketing baby formula in unsuitable conditions in Africa or the World Bank funding mega-dams on the Mekong river. Approaches vary from polite lobbying, to pointed public criticism, to confrontation in the streets.

More and more of such organizations originate in the South. The Third World Network for example has offices in Asia, Africa and Latin America. It has become one of the main networks of the anti-globalization movement. Some are regional in focus: like TERRA (Towards Ecological and Regional Alliances) which brings together groups in Southeast Asia to stop the ecological carnage being visited upon the region in the name of development. Or the Asian Women's Human Rights Council that rallies the region around the negative effects of neo-liberal policies on women.

There are two major reasons for this explosion of democratic initiatives on the global stage. One is that many of the issues faced are international in both cause and potential solution. Everything from global warming to the trade in smuggled endangered tiger- and bear- parts demands action across borders if anything substantial is to change. Who can imagine trying to stop the international arms trade only from Manhattan?

The other stimulus for international grassroots actions is to act as a check on and a counterweight to the international actors in the global economy – the transnationals and the multilateral development institutions like the World Bank which facilitate their operation. If struggles against global powerholders such as the IMF and Nike were restricted by national boundaries, an already difficult battle would become impossible. ∎

Brennan and other defenders of a revived national sovereignty believe that despite the overall record of nation-states being highly complicit in globalization, they still represent the single best hope for people to assert their democratic rights.

International problems

Most of the advocates of a cosmopolitan democracy (the term is from UK political theorist David Held) recognize these obstacles to extending democracy.[6] They simply believe there is no choice. Part of their analysis comes from an abiding distrust of the democratic credentials of the nation-state. Where nation-states are democratic at all it is by-and-large a model of weak democracy with a political class well-shielded from popular pressure that holds sway. Their inadequacy is exacerbated by the increasing number of issues – refugees, toxic pollution, the arms trade, international financial speculation and illegal commerce, global warming, tax evasion, the debt burden of poor countries, a number of public health issues and shifting patterns of production – that lie outside the borders of any particular nation-state. The cosmopolitan democrats have lent new cogency to the simple critique that the nation-state is 'too big for small problems, and too small for big problems.'

Even critics of the UN such as Phyllis Bennis don't think the world can do without it: 'However flawed the UN of the mid-1990s may be, the US should be pressed to support it financially and politically – not by reneging on billions in dues and destroying agencies that criticize or even diverge from the US position. The call from civil society should be one of championing the global organization – for the stark reason that there is nothing else to provide a multilateral voice for the majority of the world's countries – and sometimes, albeit rarely, for the world's people.'

Bennis sees the path of extending democracy into the international sphere as running right through the

UN system: 'UN democracy means re-empowering the UN General Assembly, fighting for broader representation in the Security Council and less power for its veto-wielding permanent members. It means demanding that the UN reclaim its right to oversee – and overturn – the decisions of the Bretton Woods Organizations, so that global macro-economic policy is not set by the wealthy countries alone.'[7]

While Bennis looks to the UN, there are myriad other schemes for extending democracy beyond the nation-state, everything from traditional World Federalism to Pan-African and Pan-Arab ideas. There has been a rebirth of interest in Pan-Africanism in particular because of the poor fit between the colonial imposition of the nation-state form with that continent's rich diversity and geography. Africa has been plagued by secessionist movements, a poor record on minority rights, many border disputes and a strong tendency towards authoritarianism and military seizures of power. All have taken their toll on the poorest most fragile part of the global South. Small wonder there is a lively and growing interest in different political forms for African democracy. The new African Union is perhaps the first tentative interest in Pan-Africanist initiatives since the formation of the Organization of African Unity.

The European model

The most developed model of a regionalized democracy is that represented by European integration. Unlike other integration movements such as the Free Trade Area of the Americas (FTAA) and the Asia-Pacific Economic Conference (APEC), the Europeans have gone beyond economic liberalization to try and balance the economic with representative political institutions and extending the rights of the ordinary citizen. Europe has an elected parliament (elected by proportional representation) in Strasbourg with some important powers, continent-wide tribunals whose decisions on matters of human rights and the environment are more than merely advisory, mechanisms for dealing with cultural recognition and regional disparities, and a 'social charter' that at least begins to address questions of poverty and equality. European integration allows the free movement of labor while the FTAA and APEC are only concerned with the free movement of capital and trade. Certainly it has not been all smooth sailing. There has been a tendency towards over-bureaucratization and corruption particularly in the EU administrative headquarters in Brussels. This has tarnished the young European experiment. And while the social rights enshrined in Europe are a start they are not yet strong enough to counterbalance the powers accruing to transnational investors due to economic liberalization.

Still, the new Europe remains the best hope for nationalities and regions sitting uncomfortably within existing nation-states – the Catalans and Basques in Spain, the Bretons, Basques and Corsicans in France, the Scots, Irish and Welsh in the UK – for greater autonomy and self-determination.

Cosmopolitan democracy

An ambitious scheme for extending democracy beyond the nation-state comes from the political theorist David Held. Held's 'cosmopolitan model of democracy' would extend accountability to the growing number of power centers and networks that now escape the jurisdiction of the nation-state in the globalizing economy. It is a layered approach that involves deliberative institutions at all levels and a renewal of citizen participation as a badly needed tonic for democratic political culture. Held sees an international civil society as one starting point and impetus for this. He puts heavy emphasis on a further development and enforcement of international law and regulation to rein in the arbitrary use of extra-national power. He calls for a principle of self-determination at all levels with representative and deliberative bodies globally, regionally, nationally and locally. He clearly sees economic regulation with the goal of greater equality-based outcomes as a central principle. This is a clear departure from the economic liberalization agenda of 'leaving it all up to the market.' Some such initiatives are already under way as the ATTAC movement tries to bring in an international tax on currency speculation. Others are formulating a 'bit' tax on the profits of international telecommunications that escape 'capture' by national tax authorities.

Held knows such proposals are ambitious and will not come easily. 'While the circumstances are clearly fraught with danger, and the risk of an intensification of a sectarian politics, they also present a new possibility: the recovery of an intensive and participatory democracy at local levels as a complement to the deliberative and representative assemblies of the wider global order. That is, they contain the possibility of a political order of democratic associations, workplaces and cities as well as nations, regions and global networks.'[8] So Held stands on the ground of extending democracy simultaneously both downwards to the local and upwards to the global. Such a visionary proposal would end the monopoly of the nation-state as the sole significant site for democratic deliberation.

Whatever the merits of either a reinvigorated nation-state or the extension of democracy into the international sphere the problem of unaccountable global power has to be addressed. For the future of democracy is starting to look pretty grim. Our weak-willed political class perched in isolated nation-states and blinded by a globalist vision of a brave new world is simply no match for the large corporations and the international bureaucracies that are facilitating that vision. This political class has proved all too willing to join a 'race to the bottom' (in environmental standards, wages, social programs, the quality of life) in order to compete for trade and investment capital. It seems to matter little to them what their various electorates actually want.

The nation-state advocates are accused of standing for a dubious nostalgia that history has already passed by. Those who advocate an internationalizing of democracy are accused of abandoning its best defense with a wild jump into the future that is at bottom a kind of capitulation to corporate globalization. This polarization is probably not useful. It seems likely that some kind of hybrid strategy that affirms people's right to decide on all levels needs to emerge from this debate. It makes little sense to fight for strong democracy only or mainly on one level. The energy and imagination of the anti-globalization movement faces a multilevel world of power with the central axis of the whole system running through Washington and New York. It needs a multi-pronged process of democratic action that entrenches popular power in local communities and regions but also projects it onto the national and international stage.

1 'Women, democracy and the future of nations', Marjorie Cohen in *States Against Markets*, eds Boyer and Drache, Routledge, London 1996. **2** Cohen, op cit. **3** *Calling the Shots*, Phyllis Bennis, Olive Branch Press, New York 1996. **4** Bennis, op.cit. **5** 'Cosmopolitanism and Internationalism', Timothy Brennan, in *New Left Review* Jan/Feb 2001. **6** *Democracy and the Global Order*, David Held, Polity Press, Cambridge 1995. **7** Bennis, op. cit. **8** Held, op. cit.

6 Democratizing democracy

'The cure for the problems of democracy is more democracy.'
John Dewey, philosopher.

The popular discontents of our model of weak democracy have undercut confidence not just in those we elect but in government itself. This has rebounded to the benefit of those who would leave everything up to the market. Debate rages as to how to restore popular faith in democracy. This chapter looks at such issues as direct democracy, decentralism and greater proportionality that could breathe life into ossified democratic structures.

JOHN DEWEY, the renowned American pragmatist philosopher, did famous battle with Walter Lippmann – a notable champion of weak democracy. Dewey held out for a more profound democratic citizenship in which the people were fully-fledged democratic subjects that shaped the public realm. For Lippman, democracy was all about technique and the arts of political manipulation. He helped shape the tactics of Woodrow Wilson, who after being elected US President on a pledge to keep the country out of World War One, reversed himself and dragged Americans into the slaughter of the trenches. 'Saying one thing and then doing the other' has since become almost the norm for the political class.

Dewey was appalled, but Lippmann placed himself on the side of those trying to 'manage' democracy. He concentrated on the 'arts of persuasion' and consensus-building, on technique and the details of exercising power.

It was a dispute that by-and-large it is safe to say Lippmann won in practice whatever the merits of his case. Orthodox political science has become preoccupied with exit polls, interest groups, precinct by precinct voting and the mechanisms for exercising power. As the 20th century wore on, political theorists became preoccupied with the totalitarian enemies of democracy (fascism, communism, fundamentalism) and spent little time critically examining the democracy they were defending. This is today slowly changing as the theorists of democracy are recognizing the malaise that is starting to paralyze the system. It is heartening to see the wide diversity of ideas and programs to deepen democracy that are now starting to appear.

Direct democracy

Perhaps the purest form of democracy is the direct democracy that we inherited from the Athenian city-state. It is decidedly out of fashion today. For most of

Strong democracy: letting people decide

Direct referenda have mostly been used to decide major constitutional issues. The number of such votes increased dramatically in the last quarter of the 20th century. The Danes decided not to join the common European currency. The Scots and the Welsh decided to have their own parliaments. The Quebecois decided not to leave Canada. The Chileans decided that they had had enough of military rule. Most Eastern Europeans decided on the kind of post-Communist political system they wanted. The New Zealanders decided how to change their voting system. The Spanish voted on a new constitution. While some of these results overturned the recommendations of the political élite, most were soberly taken after thoughtful debate.

Only in a few countries – about half the US states, Italy and most prominently Switzerland – are referenda and voter initiative used to consult the public on non-constitutional issues. Referenda are usually organized from above by the government while citizen initiative (such as anti-gun laws passed in some US eastern states) are initiated from below by groups of citizens and civil society organizations. In Italy initiatives backed by the Catholic Church that would have thrown out divorce and abortion were rejected by Italian voters. So was an automatic cost-of-living wage increase supported by the Communists.

These kind of initiatives are often supported by 'new groups' those who study and engage in politics, any notion of direct democracy is a dangerously utopian one that easily slides into demagoguery and populist intolerance.

But can we realistically expect active citizenship without at least some experience of direct democracy? Indeed in the associations of civil society beyond the state – everything from the vendors' association in Kampala's central market in Uganda, to the Girl Scouts of Indianapolis – engage ordinary people in making directly democratic decisions. They decide rules, define membership, vote on budgets, argue over policy. Literally millions of people around the world – everywhere from communist Cuba to free-market Switzerland – are thus engaged.

Without their participation it is scarcely possible to imagine how society would run at all. If it were left to a class of politicians directing a professional bureau-

---

(feminists, environmentalists) or smaller political parties (Greens in Switzerland, the Radical Party in Italy) as a way of putting their issues before the public. Some concrete results have been electoral reform in Italy and a moratorium on nuclear power in Switzerland. Groups in the US have pushed for everything from tax reform to legalizing the medical use of marijuana.

Since the 1850s there have been nearly five hundred national referenda in Switzerland. They are held on up to four days every year. Some three quarters have been called by the government itself with the remaining 25 per cent being initiated from below. The number of such votes is on the increase.

The Swiss have voted on budget allocations, military spending, immigration policy, their relationship to Europe and countless other matters. Hundreds of other referenda and initiatives have taken place at the Swiss Canton (Regional) government level often about public expenditure and planning and development issues. The results are far from predictable but the politics of public choice is the main beneficiary. Switzerland with a population of 6.5 million people remains a relatively wealthy and conservative country. While the lack of economic democracy restricts the full development of Swiss political life, the direct forms of participation prove that letting the people decide is no pipe dream. ∎

cracy to run all social organizations – the inefficiencies and the cost would be unimaginable. Citizens also
engage in direct action as a form of political participation. This is often the means chosen by the young
and the marginalized, who have given up on the electoral opportunities provided by a weak representative
democracy. Their attempts to influence the course of
events from the streets are often treated by the political class as unfortunate disruptions to orderly
decision-making or even as terroristic threats to the
very idea of democracy. In fact new issues – minority
rights or environmental protection – can often only
enter the political arena through direct action and
demonstrations. A complacent political class has at
best a lukewarm interest in new issues and significant
changes.

Restricted participation

Any meaningful direct democracy is by-and-large
excluded from the political sphere. The reasons put
forward for the impossibility of direct democracy
sound a lot like the ideas that used to be marshaled
against any democracy at all: 'The people are not
educated enough, are too apathetic, too easily misled
by demagogues, issues are too complex, the knowledge needed is too detailed and can only be grasped
by experts, population size is too large, decisions need
to be taken quickly and there is not enough time for
lengthy democratic consultation.'

There is of course partial truth to some of this but it
is also a failure of imagination and design. For one
thing the current apathetic voter or non-voter can only
be transformed and educated by actually participating.
Under existing circumstances the malaise discussed in
Chapter 2 can only deepen. An interest in public affairs
and a thirst for knowledge to inform thoughtful decisions will never come as long as decisions remain
beyond the reach of the ordinary citizen. In politics, as
elsewhere in life, learning comes with doing.

Experiments in direct democracy

Where elements of direct democracy have survived (some US states, Switzerland, a number of other localities that periodically allow their voters to speak directly) it is by no means clear that the quality of decisions is worse than if they had been taken by the political class. While there have been some unfortunate decisions, in such areas as taxes and immigrants' rights, there have been courageous ones on the medical use of marijuana and environmental protection. Direct democratic decision-making has proved in practice to be neither consistently reactionary nor colored by thoughtless populist reaction.

In some cases, such as the Canadian referendum on the Charlottetown Accords to revise the Constitution in the early 1990s, voters rejected the view held by virtually the entire political class from Right to Left and turned down what they felt to be a threat to the capacity of the national government to enforce standards across the country. It is by no means clear that they were wrong about this. Politicians are often unpleasantly surprised when they try and use direct democracy as a mere tool of manipulation. A good example is the refusal of the Chilean people, once given the chance, to endorse General Pinochet's military dictatorship. If anything, initiatives of direct democracy have been marked by a healthy measure of thoughtfulness and even skepticism on the part of the public.

Greater direct democracy remains an important source of inspiration and ideas in the attempt to stiffen the backbone of a weak democracy where decisions are increasingly out of the hands of the majority. The political writer Ian Budge, whose pioneering work has helped revive interest in direct democracy, believes that it can be creatively combined with representative democracy. Budge thinks it possible to supplement out-of-touch parliaments and political parties with a regularized popular mandate where voters would

Strong democracy:
can NGOs be democratic?

In the early 1970s Oxfam-Canada underwent a profound transformation. Inspired by an understanding of the political nature of what was then known as 'underdevelopment' a core group of Oxfam volunteers and staff fought an internal battle that altered the organization. The conventional top-down organization supporting apolitical 'gifts to the poor' no longer seemed appropriate. The changed Oxfam was something not very familiar in the non-governmental organization (NGO) world. Salaries were flatlined so every one made the same money. The organization committed itself to a project of self-management – the shared responsibility of staff and volunteer activists. Radical decentralization meant much more power for regional boards and local committees across the country; much less in Ottawa. Power flowed very much from the bottom up. The external policy was shaped to link popular struggles in the South with those in the North; the understanding being that only a transformation of our own societies could significantly alter unequal power relations that shaped global inequalities.

To achieve this Oxfam not only shifted its support towards popular movements in the South but also undertook to support popular education, poor and anti-racist organizations and challenges to corporate-led development in Canada. Over the years the organization devoted hundreds of thousands of donors' dollars to this work and did not shy away from the innovative task of public fund-raising for these campaigns.

Such a bold shift in direction was not without its problems and discontents. The decision-making process for a radically decentralized national organization can be long and frustrating. No one was ever willing to take someone else's word simply because of the position they held in the organization. Meetings dragged on. The public perception of the organization changed slowly. While core supporters were brought along the mass influx of money and new supporters that came from disaster relief was harder to sustain. The media still maintained the conventional view of Oxfam as a development charity and shaped public expectations in that direction. The role of a development NGO was after all to transform as many donors' dollars as possible to food in the mouths of hungry people tomorrow or at least the day after. Relations with government, including the Canadian International Development Agency, became strained and suspicious over everything from political engagement to bureaucratic reporting norms. Oxfam didn't shy away from controversial public statements. Oxfam-Canada was involved in a delicate and innovative balancing act to maintain its traditional charity functions while also taking on many of the characteristics of a social movement. To maintain its democratic ambitions, it had to sustain this balance and not fall off the beam in either direction.

Gradually the cobwebs of contradiction started to gather. There was a growing frustration of those in 'managerial' roles that their ability to manage was being hampered by too much democratic consultation and they were not being adequately rewarded for their professional credentials and responsibilities. Other staff pushed to unionize (to some degree in response), short-circuiting their own role as self-managers for that of militant workers. Money became short (due to a large degree to ill-thought-out investments in a trading company) and people started to look around for places to cut. The regional boards (too costly and time-wasting) and the domestic program (not a good fund-raiser) were obvious targets. In those years many expensive consultants came and went and advice flowed freely.

Gradually Oxfam-Canada was forced back into a more conventional mold. Regionalization was abandoned in favor of a process of volunteer 'units' and 'unit assemblies' who meet infrequently enough so that any real policy input or oversight of the organization is difficult. Regional boards were dissolved. The numbers of volunteers were restricted to a few at the National Board level (who seldom discuss program) and then those around the units. Volunteers who used to make up a vital part of program development and choices are now largely absent. Their role has been taken by professional staff. While many are still committed to support for popular movements in the South, there has been a cost. Cutbacks have largely wiped out the resources Oxfam-Canada used to provide to support popular education and social struggles in Canada. Staff in the regions and in charge of Oxfam's Canadian Program have been cut back while the Ottawa office has expanded. The 'professionalization' of the organization has been achieved at the cost of a vital internal democratic life. Many dedicated staff are still committed to the political goals set out by Oxfam but must now pursue them in the context of a professional development agency that has shed many of its characteristics of a democratic movement.

Oxfam-Canada now more closely resembles a conventional NGO model. But the context in which Oxfam operates has changed. Now the 1970s' analysis of 'political poverty' is widely shared amongst other NGOs and a growing anti-globalization movement in the country. The democratic experiment in Oxfam helped shape this new context. The fate of Oxfam-Canada does however show how difficult it is to create 'democracy' in a situation of constantly swimming against the current. When expectations of the government, the casual donor, the media and an ideology of professionalism all run to the contrary, it is easy for the sources of democratic imagination to dry up. ■

endorse or reject significant policy proposals put forward by party-based governments. According to Budge, in this scenario 'parliament would change into an advisory, investigative and debating committee informing popular discussion and voting, rather than substituting for it.'[1] This could provide a popular check on the wild swings in policy and the influence of powerful extra-parliamentary groups on the professional political class. History might be quite different if acts like the declaration of war or the imposition of widespread structural adjustment programs in the South could not be implemented without first seeking a popular mandate.

Budge goes on to paint a picture of a reinvigorated and lively political culture under direct democracy: 'If a special organization were dedicated to ensuring fair electronic coverage of policy discussions, this could relay initial debate in parliament and possibly the proceedings of commissions of inquiry on the Swedish model; then go onto party broadcasts, deliberative discussion by representative samples and juries, transmission of local meetings, phone-ins, questions and comments to national media. In other words the whole gamut of current coverage should be systematically organized on a regular basis.'[2]

More thoughtful decisions

Critics claim that direct democracy would slow down the process of government. But this might just as easily be seen as a significant advantage. Policy decisions taken in haste are often regretted at leisure. Greater caution might temper the headlong rush towards an unthinking growth trampling all obstacles and non-economic values in its path. It might also be a useful counterbalance to the egoism and self-enrichment of political leaders or the *raison d'état* so popular with the bureaucrats. Too often the prerogatives of the national security state are asserted as an automatic reflex to cut off more thoughtful debate.

The extension of democracy to direct decision-making can be seen as a continuation of the decades of struggle to expand the franchise to all citizens. This bitter battle was won only after some very hard-fought campaigns from below. The struggle for a fair franchise was opposed with predictions of catastrophe, so we should not be surprised to hear such claims again. But on the evidence of a few US states and the Swiss example it would seem likely that popular mandate would have protected health and educational services better and done more for the environment. Budge and other advocates of increased direct democracy put great stock in the development of a network of interactive new technology-based media to facilitate broader-based democratic decisions.

This raises significant questions of access, ownership, cost and the potential manipulation of such media. But it also promises direct popular control without the bogey of endless boring meetings. Mass society can obviously not revert to a classical Athenian model of large town-hall type gatherings – although this method of local input could still play an important role in any decentralized political system. Neighborhood-type budget meetings in the communities of the Brazilian city of Porto Alegre have played a large role in creating a truly participatory municipal budget. In small towns, Majority World villages, and urban neighborhoods this kind of decision-making could prove quite appropriate.

But whatever the method, the apathy and withdrawal of people from political life can only be overcome with meaningful participation and the growth of interactive technologies cannot but aid such a possibility. Already mass demonstrations like that against the World Trade Organization in Seattle and many other significant political movements have found a virtual meeting place on the world wide web.

There is a modest but growing revival of interest in direct democracy. There are advocacy groups in many countries and biannual conventions of the Committee for Direct Democracy. They are encouraged by the possibilities presented by interactive new technologies in which they see the potential of a much greater amount of democratic deliberation and input. It is likely that the parts of the South (particularly rural areas) where there are indigenous traditions of popular decision-making could form the basis of a direct democracy there.

Limited representation

It is hard to imagine a working democracy that does not involve representative forms, whatever the mix with direct consultation of voters and popular initiative from below. This opens up the question of what kind of 'representation'. The current system is one where we are represented in public political life by one or two sets of professional politicians – depending on whether we live under federal or unitary systems. These politicians are organized in 'more or less' democratic political parties. Such parties run the ideological spectrum from Right to Left (although here differences between them are certainly narrowing). Some may represent particular regions or interests. The most successful have generally been the big brokerage parties – the Democrats and the Republicans in the US, the Liberal Democratic Party in Japan, the old Congress Party of India, the Liberal Party in Canada or the PRI party in Mexico. Such parties have loose ideological commitments and use a vaguely populist rhetoric (often of the Left) while campaigning. They typically contain a number of powerful factions and interest groups each of which stakes a claim on policy and economic awards once the party is in power.

Parties of a more ideological stripe (say Labour in Britain) are gradually transforming themselves into this kind of 'brokerage' party in the depoliticized climate of market democracy. The kind of 'representation' one can hope to get from such parties (especially in situations where they monopolize power) is limited by the number of claims of other powerful stakeholders and the extra-parliamentary corporate power embedded in the capitalist economy. The conditions under which a majority government governs have been variously described as 'an elective dictatorship' or in British cultural critic Raymond Williams's telling phrase 'the periodic election of a court'.

Williams traces the various notions of representation from the time of the Estates-General in revolutionary France where representation was a function of social position to our notion that the elected 'represent' a geographic locality. While he grants a limited truth to such notions of representation, Williams goes on to champion 'an alternative idea of making present, in continuing and interactive ways, the various interests of those who are... represented.'[3] In other words, a regular system of accountability beyond the current arrangement of infrequent elections.

Under most present circumstances these 'representatives' are only answerable to us in a very general sense. Once they have been elected any number of factors may weigh more heavily for them than the wishes of their constituents; their own views, Party discipline, personal ambition or the influence of powerful lobbies. Voters by-and-large do not get to hold them accountable until the next general election. In the meantime they form a virtual dictatorship – particularly if they are part of a majority government. Even this meager exercise of the popular will implied by elections must overcome a multiplicity of unrepresentative forms (unelected houses like the British Lords or the Canadian Senate, religious chambers like that which stymies the Iranian parliament, the US Electoral College) which are designed to provide a buffer against unpredictable public opinion.

The very language of politics reveals how little 'representation' means in practice. A newly-elected leader often makes the claim that they will put partisanship behind them and will from now on set themselves the task of representing 'all the people'. This is of course ridiculous and insulting to those who worked against them in the election and are absolutely opposed to their program. It is also insulting to those who believe in their program and supported them in the election.

Then there is the case of an unelected but prominent member of the political class – a leader who does not hold a seat, a promising candidate for a high-level job new to party politics, the offspring or spouse of a well-known political dynasty. The cry goes up that 'they must be found a seat'. Some local representative is then pushed to resign so that the celebrity can stand in their place. In what sense can such a person be said to 'represent' their new constituents?

This remains a source of irritation for those who hold to democratic principles on both the political Left and the political Right. The former see the inequalities in the rest of society biasing representation towards the already powerful while the latter see a bureaucratic state remote from the control of the ordinary citizen. Certainly more direct democracy would act as a popular check. A plethora of ideas for greater empowerment of and participation by ordinary citizens just won't go away. These take a variety of forms. Referenda over key questions, recall of individual representatives or entire governments, variations on the voting system, decentralization, town hall meetings, term limits to prevent a political class from entrenching itself, federalism, deliberative democracy involving citizen juries – the list for revitalizing democracy is almost endless. The thread that runs through all such proposals is to put the people back in the democratic picture.

The proportionality debate

The actual electoral system plays a big role in determining how well citizens feel represented. Unlike systems of proportional representation (PR) where it is easier to express minority views, the 'first-past-the-post' (FPTP) system tends to produce two or at the most three largish 'consensus' political parties grouped around the Center-Left or the Center-Right. It is a situation in which the brokerage parties described above flourish. Countries currently using FPTP include India, Canada, the US, the UK and with some variation, France. It is exceptionally hard for new parties with different ideas (a Green Party for example) to break through the political monopoly of FPTP. In the FPTP system if I vote for a candidate whom I know will not win in my riding or constituency, my vote is simply wasted. In systems based on proportionality all votes end up counting towards the final result and are not 'wasted'.

In most European electoral systems such votes are tallied as part of the overall national result and help elect a group of MPs to parliament that express each voter's preference. This allows people to vote more with their 'conscience' and according to their desires rather than being put in a position of having to choose tactically the lesser of evils to ensure their votes will count. It is noteworthy that most of the systems of Eastern Europe and other societies like South Africa that have recently had the opportunity to shape new electoral systems have chosen some form of proportional representation rather than FPTP systems.

The FPTP system is favored by the economic establishment and many political scientists because it trades democracy and minority views for political stability. There is often a conservative bias in favor of strong economic medicine and hard choices that a 'tough' leadership must take. This is however mixing up democratic principle with a desired policy outcome. The purpose of an electoral system is to 'represent' as accurately as possible the wishes of the voters. The messy multiparty coalitions that are more typical of PR may not lend themselves to boss-type politicians like

Margaret Thatcher or Ronald Reagan but they have consistently shown a higher degree of citizen involvement and interest.

Just a few statistics will give a sense of the bias built into FPTP. In the 1997 campaign the winning British Labour Party got 63.4 per cent of the parliamentary seats with only 43.2 per cent of the popular vote. By contrast in the last Russian election under a variation

Strong democracy: local self-government

Three times the council of the beautiful British Columbia foothill town of Rossland brought their salary increase before the 12,000 odd citizens of the town. Three times the citizens said no. Rossland is one of the few municipalities where the citizens have this power. Inspired by municipal administrator Andre Carrel, Rossland in 1990 passed its own municipal constitution bylaw which allows for a system of referendum and citizens' initiative. The idea was simple and revolutionary. 'All bylaws should be subject to citizens' consent, implied or expressed, at the discretion of citizens themselves, not only where the law (or council) deemed it appropriate.' In other words the citizens in Rossland were engaged in the profoundest expression of strong democracy – self-rule.

The people of Rossland used their new powers to push through dramatic improvements in water quality approving Can$4 million (US$2.5m/£1.7m) to establish British Columbia's largest slow sand water filtration and first ozone water disinfection plant. It established a Water Quality Reserve based on a new property tax. Drinking water quality has become a major issue in Canada since the poisoning of over a thousand citizens of Walkerton, Ontario due to irresponsible provincial downloading and privatization. The people of Rossland also approved fire and recreational facilities back under municipal control in order to control expenditure and program quality. There was no generalized tax-slashing and program-gutting that critics of direct democracy so feared. Carrel reports that attitudes towards local government have undergone a profound shift in Rossland. 'The damned government' excuse has lost much of its credibility, because municipal policy decisions are either approved directly by a majority of the citizenry through referenda, or they are consented to by their abstention. Governing under the umbrella of a municipal constitution, citizens have defined the policy fence within which their council may govern their municipality.

Sounds good but it is all illegal. Canadian towns and cities do not have the power to govern themselves either directly or indirectly. Like most municipalities in other parts of the world, Canadian local of PR the Communist Party took 25.6 per cent of the seats with 24.3 per cent of the vote. FPTP has left a few very powerful and well-funded political parties – the Republicans and the Democrats in the US, The Labour Party and Tories in the UK, the Liberal Party in Canada – to dominate. Canada presents the classic case of a country both regionally and politically balkanized by the first-past-the-post electoral system. Most

government is simply a creation of those levels of government (in the Canadian case provinces) immediately above them. The treatment of London's Greater London Council by the Thatcher Government in the UK provides graphic evidence of the colonial status of municipal government there. Canadian provincial governments can and have dissolved municipalities, altered their taxing powers, changed their boundaries, reduced the number of elected representatives they can have and downloaded service responsibilities from higher levels of government. Most Canadian major cities have either undergone or are undergoing a brutal process of amalgamation with their suburbs whether they want to or not. In Canada's largest city, Toronto, over 70 per cent of the electorate in a referendum voted against amalgamation but it was imposed by the Conservative provincial government anyway.

The subordinate status of local government is a severe impediment to true democracy. Andre Carrel believes that the colonial status of municipalities needs to be challenged if democracy is not going to continue to deteriorate into a mass of disgruntled consumers rather than citizens. The 'one size fits all' municipal policies of higher levels of government deny the uniqueness of every municipality's problems and potential solutions. Carrel sees Rossland's experiment in direct democracy not so much as a blueprint that other places could copy but as a source of inspiration for doing things differently. A political contract between local government and its citizenry to seek not just consultation but also direct approval is very much a question of political will. Carrel feels that the demands for directly democratic alternatives will only grow in the present context. He concludes that 'The idea of citizen empowerment is a powerful thing. As more governments strive to become "mean and lean" as public policy is increasingly determined by economic policy and as economic policy is increasingly shaped in global terms, interest in meaningful citizen participation in decisions that will alter the community will grow.' This places the fight for municipal self-governance directly in the path of the steamroller of globalization.

Taken from *Citizens' Hall: making local democracy work*, by Andre Carrel, Between the Lines 2001. ∎

political parties are under-represented in the House of Commons with MPs drawn only from particular regions (although most have support across the country). The Liberal Party of Canada on the other hand maintains a vast majority in parliament despite a popular vote hovering only around the 40 per cent mark. Frustration among Canadians can be seen in a decreased membership in political parties and an increased refusal to vote.

Control from below

While proportionality in the electoral system may be part of the answer it will not satisfy the requirements of a fully-fledged democracy that values self-rule. Indeed if a PR system is not modified by internal party democracy it will replicate many of the problems of the FPTP system with élite negotiations between sectors of the political class far removed from popular control. Strains in the German and other Green parties (as they participate in government) are already starting to show up.

The requirements for a deepened democracy can be introduced through integrating elements of direct rule into the system. Other elements of democratic reform – terms limits, citizen juries and assemblies, recall provisions – may also be useful. But unlike the basic formula of 'weak democracy/strong market' that the advocates of globalization are trying to install from Luanda to Liverpool, it is important to avoid a 'one size fits all' approach to democratic reform. There are sources of democratic strength in everything from the emerging civil society in autocratic China to indigenous consensual decision-making in Andean Latin America. Democratic practice in a dense urban area (popular neighborhood assemblies and so on) is likely to be very different from democracy in a desert region of relatively sparse population. Each society must find strengths in its own traditions and shape a sense of 'representation' based on its own needs rather than simply importing the Western model of a weak democracy. This will involve active resistance to the ideological pressures to adopt a US model as the only 'real' democracy.

In a variety of rich forms however the notion of who 'represents' us cries out to be broadened. Where we cannot 'represent' ourselves through direct voting on important policies or participation in local assemblies we may still need to be represented. But this representation does not have to be by a few members of a more-or-less permanent political class operating from offices in some remote capital. Instead we need a rich variety of representation in our housing co-ops, workplaces, neighborhoods, schools and universities, regional planning boards or environmental advisory committees. This is the only way to really democratize contemporary life. This implies a radical decentralization of power based on the principle that all decisions should be taken by those most directly concerned with them. A policy of maximum self-management could enrich and enliven, educate and animate democratic practice. Democracy would no longer feel like something remote monopolized by a few 'all purpose' representatives but part of everyday life where citizens had regular interactions with those that were charged with carrying out their wishes.

1 *The New Challenge of Direct Democracy*, Ian Budge, Polity Press, Cambridge 1996. **2** op. cit. **3** *The Year 2000*, Raymond Williams, Pantheon Books, New York 1983.

7 Democracy and ecology

'Find your place on the planet, dig in, and take responsibility from there.'

Gary Snyder, poet.

The environmental crisis is challenging orthodox democracy in some very crucial ways. A market democracy where real democratic power is traded for an ever-expanding consumer prosperity is just not sustainable. The short time frames most politicians work from cannot cope with the long term impacts of ecological change. This chapter sorts through the toolkit of Green ideas for building an eco-democracy where environmental health is a first principle.

THE ENVIRONMENTAL DIMENSION is something relatively new for democratic thinkers to cope with. Classical democratic theory just assumed a bountiful nature where endless free goods were there for human enjoyment. They simply needed to be transformed into private property or were nature's free 'inputs' into the creation of commodities. But in today's world of collapsing ecosystems, shrinking resources and the widespread dispersal of toxins the situation is very different.

Environmental issues have become a major focus of democratic action. John Locke or Jean-Jacques Rousseau could never have imagined the Chipko movement in the Himalayas trying to defend their forest resources and watersheds (and livelihood) against commercial logging interests. Nor could they have put themselves on the streets of Southern megacities like Mexico City and Bangkok where breathable air is at a premium. Environmental issues if they existed at all were local; the potentially catastrophic impact of unsustainable human activity on the global climate was simply unimaginable.

Whether it is endangered species and bioregions or desertification and the growing scarcity of usable water, environmental problems and issues amount to a major new challenge for democratic theory. How best to husband resources, minimize eco-impacts and slow a sustainable growth to manageable proportions presents a significant challenge to democracy. In the weak democracy/strong market model the sovereign consumer is king – unless of course your income (or lack thereof) fails to translate into effective demand. The 'buy, buy, buy' ethos has a very strong hold on popular consciousness. It has the potential of pitting a consumerist majority on one side against a minority on the other who see the need to get off this unsustainable treadmill. Environmentalists are easily portrayed as people who want to 'spoil the party'. It is a classic challenge of minority/majority relations.

Short time frames

Environmentalists also face the problem of the 'time frame' of democratic politics as currently practised. The politician must promise jobs and prosperity on a very short time frame – with elections occurring every four or five years at most. Given our personality-based politics, with little substantive discussion of issues (on average in the US a politician takes eight seconds to answer a question) the coinage of success in modern electoral campaigns often hangs on who promises to deliver 'the goods' most efficiently.

Although it is usually best to coat such practicalities as some kind of 'vision thing' it is really a kind of meat-and-potatoes politics. Questions of incremental climate change occurring over decades, the gradual extinction of plant and animal species or our obligation to leave future generations a liveable world are difficult to turn into media sound-bites. Politics as practised makes it difficult to turn such concerns into effective political programs. The fact that we are pushing a hundred species a day into evolutionary oblivion just never registers in the opinion polls. The Bush regime's abandoning of its commitments to the already minimalist Kyoto Accords on global climate change is typical. A whole generation of politicians has put off meaningful commitments to environmental protection because they just don't see any votes in it. A more deliberative participatory democracy which engages people as citizens and not just consumers would be no guarantee of better results, but it could hardly do worse. A slowed-down democracy allowing more time for deliberation and popular input would allow more space than the frenetic 'silly season' of our current electoral campaigns.

Consumerism over citizenship

Eco-politics has tackled the question of democracy in a number of ways. Green political thinking tends to see contemporary society as suffering from a crisis of participation. According to this logic citizens have withdrawn from public life and involvement and replaced these engagements with the pleasures of shopping and various passive entertainments. People have in a sense abdicated their role as citizens and make up for their powerlessness in the public arena through these compensatory activities – jet skis, all-terrain 4-wheel-drive vehicles, computer paraphernalia and the latest logo clothing. It is hard to know what came first – the pleasures of consumerism or the powerlessness associated with the 'weak democracy' model. Most Green political philosophy puts at the center of its concerns a revival of popular participation and a trade-off between a richer quality of life (more power, less time working, a more democratic culture) against a reduction in the quantity of life (low energy lifestyles and a reduction of conspicuous consumption). One form that participation could then take is to safeguard and renovate the natural world.

Tied to this notion of participation is a more-or-less

radical advocacy of decentralism. Green political theory has a strain running through it that almost inevitably favors the decentralization of democratic decisions. The degree of decentralism is cause for heated debate within the various currents of Green thought. Some, like the fundamentalist factions that exist in most Green parties or the eco-anarchists and bioregionalists, believe that all society must revert to a simpler form and scale if we are to survive as a species. Their emphasis is then to create the forms of this new society that can live in harmony with their local ecosystem and defend it if necessary from corporate or other degradation. Eventually this would involve changing patterns of human settlement so that major urban conglomerations would be broken up. Democratic decision-making then is a face-to-face matter drawing inspirations often from the tradition of indigenous peoples.

Beyond the local

Other currents of eco-politics point to the fact that many of the environmental problems facing the earth are not solvable by operating simply on a local level. People in this frame feel that issues such as climate change, our automobile culture and genetic engineering cannot be solved by concentrating power in local communities no matter how democratically they are run. Furthermore they hold that leaving the national and international arenas to powerful corporate and bureaucratic organizations would only mean that their decisions went unchallenged. They thus put forward a notion of political democracy that decentralizes many decisions currently taken at the national level.

Other decisions involving planning, national standards for air and water quality, treaties to protect the environment and so forth need to be taken at the level of regions, nation-states or even internationally. This strain of eco-politics calls for the democratization of these higher levels of politics. This is necessary not only to encourage broader participation and interest but to curb the unequal weight of those with a major stake in the current industrial system. Only then will there be a chance to restore ecological balance and healthier lives.

Southern complexities

In the South the matter is even more complicated. Ecological sentiment is often held as coming from a position of Northern privilege. While this is slowly changing as Southern environmental movements grow in strength, it is still a widely-held perception. It has not been helped by the cavalier attitude of some Northern environmentalists to the life-and-death situations many people in the South face every day. But in a situation of real (as opposed to manipulated) economic scarcity there is heavy pressure on limited resources. Poverty and the threat to actual survival can force those at the bottom into a desperate misuse of resources (seen in deforestation, soil exhaustion, water pollution).

This process is further intensified by the multi-layered pressures to integrate national economies into the global marketplace by organizing them around the uncontrolled exploitation of resources, whether it is Zambian copper or Indonesian cocoa. Highly indebted countries desperate to earn foreign exchange are not likely to listen to lectures on sound ecological practice. The last few decades have also witnessed the transfer of low-wage dirty industries to 'free trade zones' in places like Mexico and Central America, Indonesia or the Philippines. Such investment decisions are made for a number of reasons, one being to avoid diligent enforcement of environmental regulation.

Not only do these pressures of globalism and the inequalities they generate increase environmental degradation but they also significantly narrow democratic possibilities. There has been much preaching to the Majority World about the values such as 'open-ness', 'good governance' and 'democracy'. In World Bank documents or in the speeches of the political worthies of the West the case for what amounts to the strong market/weak democracy model has been made ad infinitum. The problem is that, even more than in the industrial world, the economic inequalities generated by such a system are best managed by autocratic means. The political response to these inequalities – food riots, marginalized regions seeking autonomy or independence, assertive shantytown communities or peasant organizations, trade unions wanting to break the low-wage cycle or grassroots eco-activists advocating a truly sustainable development – often have to be controlled using undemocratic and frequently heavy-handed means. Widespread crime, corruption, drugs and a 'burgeoning' underground economy further increase the tendency to use the police rather than parliament as the means of government. Majority world democracies are fragile with a narrow basis of consensus. The strong market/weak democracy model puts too much stress on both the natural environment and democratic possibilities.

Eco-democracy

In this sense the fate of the ecosystem and substantial democracy are closely linked. The defense of one increases the possibilities for the other. A decentralized environmentally-friendly approach to development could underpin a decentralized democracy where people have a real say. The political machines that compete today to divvy up the spoils and protect the system that generates such spoils mutilate democratic possibilities. Whatever the outcome of the various debates within the Green movement over the degree of direct democracy or decentralization it is hard to imagine a sustainable democracy of the future that is not green. The mounting environmental problems – climate collapse, species endangerment, chemical poisoning, resource depletion, biogenetic hazards – can never be solved by the strong market/weak democracy model.

As we saw in Chapter 3, CB Macpherson, in his pioneering work on the origins and nature of the strong market/weak democracy model, identifies the basis of the 'possessive individualism' that underpins the whole tradition of liberal democracy. Macpherson sees and critiques the classical tradition as being dependent on the idea of each individual maximizing their powers as a way of maximizing their desires. He identifies the 'infinite desire to possess and consume' as the source of power hoarding (both economic and political power) typical of market society. Writing back in the 1970s he is optimistic that society is moving towards a post-scarcity situation where the 'compulsive labor' associated with this limitless desire will no longer be necessary.[1]

From the viewpoint of the turn of the century with its triumphal capitalism, ecological crisis and persistent inequalities this seems very optimistic. Perhaps a better starting point as a new basis for democracy is Gandhi's notion that 'there is enough for everyone's need, but not for everyone's greed.' We are facing an ecological situation where 'possessive individualism' is increasingly in conflict with species survival – including our own. Any ecological democracy would clearly need to identify and reject as its basis the classic liberal notion of the right of each individual to maximize their desires and powers. This is perhaps the most promising intersection of democratic theory with green political thought.

1 *Democratic Theory: Essays in Retrieval*, CB Macpherson, Oxford University Press 1973.

8 Strong democracy in the South

> *'If you act like there is no possibility of change, you guarantee that there will be no change.'*
> **Noam Chomsky, political theorist.**

In the South democratic rights are often a life-and-death question. But they are also notoriously fragile in a situation of huge inequalities where the powerful frequently resort to brutal suppression to maintain and expand their privileges. This chapter looks at the struggle to build a more robust democracy and how it takes quite different forms based on differing national experiences. It also examines how such efforts can be side-tracked unless they are deeply embedded in popular life.

DEMOCRACY IN THE South is not yet the kind of glitzy competition between two well-oiled media machines you see in Washington or London. It is something a good deal more modest but also somehow more profound. For the Indian peasants of Andean Latin America it may simply mean that the military no longer comes to uproot their communities and livelihoods and stick them in 'strategic hamlets' for reasons of national security. In all too many places in the South it may also mean freedom from deadly raids of ethnic militias or right-wing vigilantes or getting caught in the crossfire of a dozen civil wars. It may mean for a West African civil servant a modicum of security when a change of political bosses brings in a new order. It may mean the right of environmentalists in Indonesia or Malaysia to the 'political space' necessary to put forward their case about despoiling timber resources or the polluting effects of slash-and-burn plantation practices. For an Iranian journalist it may mean the right simply to do their job in an honest fashion free from the heavy hand of self-censorship. It is often experienced as a kind of negative freedom 'from' interference, a desire to secure both personal and political space.

Freedom from, freedom to

But this 'freedom from' is inevitably connected to a 'freedom to'. For there can be little dependable 'freedom from' if there is no way in which popular power can check the activities of the authorities. In the long term this can only be guaranteed if the institutions of a grassroots democracy can shape the context in which public decisions are made. Political space depends on a lively civil society and a sense on the part of the powerful that political power is not their 'private possession' to wield as they see fit. Only a strong democracy can guarantee this. Governance powers need to pass from the central authority of the national state to the rural villages, urban communities and a variety of workplaces. Such a system of dispersed power is the only way to have a chance of giving voice to the interests and ideas of the South's poor majority.

It is here perhaps most of all that the tradition of a strong democracy is needed to bolster popular aspirations. Already these muffled voices can be heard, although they have little impact on decision-making at the peak of the national state. The bureaucratic layers of procedural habit deem them illegitimate, even subversive. But there is no denying their existence – in the fishing villages in South India, among the dissatisfied *maquila* (sweatshops) workers along the Mexican/US border, in the native communities of Sarawak or even amongst the shell-shocked refugees who have fled the deadly civil war in southern Sudan. They push up like stubborn crabgrass through the cracks in a cement sidewalk. They are the future seeds of a strong democracy: one that is responsive to the needs of poor people rather than to the dictates of corporate power. This is what makes them subversive.

Exporting democracy

As mentioned in Chapter 2 the South has in recent years (since the Cold War) been subjected to an almost constant hectoring on its undemocratic practices. Everyone from the Socialist International to the International Monetary Fund has joined the chorus. Slogans like 'good governance' and 'transparency' have become the flavor-of-the-month for the Northern advice-preaching industry. There has been a significant shift away from dictatorship and military rule to various forms of civilian rule and more-or-less freely contested elections – particularly in Latin America. Yet democratic gains remain very fragile. There are many factors that account for this. But one of underlying significance is certainly the appropriateness of the strong market/weak democracy model in conditions of extreme poverty and inequality. This model has been virtually forced onto the nation-states of the Majority World as part of a set of conditions (for credit, access to markets, favorable trade status) demanded for participation in the global economy. It is a model in which the voice of the poor majority must be restricted to the margins of political life. For if it were at the center it would threaten to overthrow the 'market logic' that is integral to this timid brand of democracy.

The instability that inevitably flows from market-generated extremes of wealth and poverty is further aggravated by various combinations of regional, ethnic or religious tensions. The headlines may speak of hostage-taking in the southern Philippines or the deadly civil war in Sri Lanka but the underlying story is one of racism, resentment and regional disparity. When causes are rooted in layers of historical complexity, solutions cannot be found in simply letting the market decide. Any democratic theory worth its salt would have it that people should be doing the deciding – not just as consumers but as citizens.

In places such as Africa the whole idea of the nation-state (the supposed site of democratic decision-making) has from the start been an uncomfortable fit – arbitrarily imposed as part of colonial history. Grouping peoples who had little in common and playing them off against each other was a part of colonial policy that Africans are still paying for. The post-colonial state as it evolved was both too top-heavy and

Strong democracy: set in stone

A stone sits at the entrance to the fishing village of Kanyakumari in the South Indian state of Tamil Nadu. It is dated 20-8-1993. It literally sets in stone a victory won by the fishworkers' union against the local trawler owners. Among other things it sets out that the trawlers are not allowed to operate during the monsoon season when fish spawn, that they must at other times return to harbor by 6 pm and not fish inside a 2-mile/5-kilometer zone from the shore which is where the artisanal fishers (the vast majority) operate.

This local law was the fruit of a hard-fought struggle between inshore fishers and trawler owners that involved such direct actions as boat captures, road blockades and hunger strikes. For the men and the increasingly active women of Kanyakumari this law carries more weight than almost anything enacted in the faraway capital of New Delhi. As one of the militant women of Kanyakumari told the provincial fisheries minister in Madras 'Our *kal vettu* (stone inscription) is the law in our village. We can't change it. If you change it, your law will remain in your office, it can't be implemented in our village.'

This was a local democratic understanding at its purest. So when the trawler-owners started to break the law – fishing in spawning season, refusing to pay for damaging the nets of inshore fishers and staying out far beyond the 6 pm limit, the community leapt into action in defense of local democracy. They marched on the local regional headquarters to demonstrate against the Collector – the highest local official largely thought to be in the pocket of the wealthy trawler-owners. The village itself became a 'no-go' area for police (they believed the threat that they would be tossed into the ocean) and actions were taken against the trawler-owners and their employees. The community had the support of the local church and branches of national fishers' organizations. Apurna Sundar reports that while many issues lacking the capacity and often the will to service its citizens. Too often the state became a means by which the already rich and powerful extracted the wealth of society for themselves. With weak infrastructure and programs, national institutions generally in Africa are not strong – except the military, which has a long and bloody history of shaping politics to meet its own ends. But the new democratic reform agenda advocated for the South by Northern experts ignores the realities of states that lack both capacity and confidence. The demand for a withdrawal by the state from both regu-

---

remain unresolved, 'the villagers did not experience the fight against trawling as a failure but as a source of empowerment. Objectively, too, it may be seen as having contributed to the building of countervailing power, the living collective consciousness of the people, their vigilance against the abuse of formal power.'

The struggle in Kanyakumari needs to be seen also as part of the overall battle that India's 8 million fishworkers have successfully fought against the carve-up of Indian waters and the licensing of foreign deep-sea fishing fleets. The fishworkers' movement spearheaded by the National Fishermen's Forum launched a national campaign against the globalization of India's fishery. Faced with shrinking catches and with no obvious economic benefits or jobs for ordinary Indians the organizers saw little choice. They used the same direct action tactics as the people of Kanyakumari with a series of national fishery strikes, blockades of major harbors and hunger strikes. They also drew on the organization of fishers in hundreds of small seaside communities like Kanyakumari to coordinate action locally and spread the word.

Another parallel between these national and local democratic struggles is the ideology of a kind of eco-democracy which emerged from both struggles. In both cases the themes of the protest were social injustice (the privilege of the few at the expense of the many), the protest against the unsustainable pillaging of the fish stocks by mechanical means and the potent argument that the food security of Indians should come before the needs of the export market. Both protests used the spaces provided by liberal democracy to expand the 'political space' for a stronger popular grassroots democracy. ∎

Information drawn from 'Sea changes: organizing around the fishery in a South Indian community' by Aparna Sundar in *Street-level Democracy* by Jonathan Barker, Between the Lines, Toronto 1999.

latory functions and basic economic protections for the marginalized will never inspire popular confidence. So the limits on democracy intrinsic to the strong market/weak democracy model simply aggravate tensions and inequalities that already afflict Majority World society.

Strong democracy

There is a tradition of struggle for a stronger democracy in the South. Elements of it can be seen in parts of the Pan-Africanist movement and in Julius Nyerere's attempts to craft an African socialism for Tanzania; the radical tradition of Bolivar, Sandino and Zapata in Latin American populism that have acted as an inspiration for both the Sandinistas of Nicaragua and the Zapatistas of southern Mexico, and currents of Gandhian direct action in South Asia. Such strong democracy traditions were smothered during the Cold War contest between market democracy (and the military dictatorships often used to preserve it) and the various forms of autocratic state socialism supported by the Soviet Union. By and large these socialisms as witnessed in places like Mengistu's Ethiopia or Pol Pot's Kampuchea (Cambodia) totally lacked any type of democratic credentials. They turned into human rights nightmares and killing grounds. Other countries such as China, Vietnam and Cuba could at least boast of some achievements in meeting people's basic needs. They are however hardly models of strong democracy. So for a whole period of post-colonial history innovation with popular forms of democracy was simply pushed off the agenda.

There is now a revival of interest in the traditions of a strong democracy. Today these blend with radical notions of indigenous self-determination, community and regional empowerment, ecological resistance, a strong civil society and economic democracy to form the fragments of an alternative to the strong market/weak democracy model. These ideas are drawing a citizenry who feel disenfranchised (whether they are allowed to cast a ballot or not) from a form of government where the tune is called in Washington or Brussels. Foreign interests work in concert with the domestic powerholders who benefit most from the globalization of the economic life. A desire for a 'strong democracy' is inspired by a growing revulsion over the gross disparities in 'life chances' between those in the walled luxury compounds of a Guatemala City or Nairobi and those clinging to existence in the urban shantytowns and marginalized villages that dot the South.

The movement to deepen democracy will inevitably look very different in different countries. Looking at another country as a model is a bad idea. Differences in activist resources, in the level of development, political traditions, and the undemocratic enemies to be faced will all shape both the struggle and the results. This is one reason why exporting US-style democracy to the rest of the world is not just self-serving but futile. Inevitably any deepening of democracy in the US will have to reshape the dominant forms of individualism in US culture and will be based on much more autonomy of the individual citizen than it would in the more collective societies of the South.

Struggles for a stronger democracy in India or Nigeria will have to draw on sources of strength (collective identities, indigenous forms of organization) that are rooted in those places.

Creating democratic space

A prerequisite for any kind of strong democracy is the popular belief that it is both desirable and possible. One source of these convictions is people's experience in running their own organizations and practising democracy on a local level. Whether it is cocoa-producer co-ops like Kuapa Kokoo in Ghana or shantytown dwellers' associations struggling to improve living conditions in Lima and Mexico City –

democratic experience helps create a confidence and belief in self-rule. Throughout the South such practices of local democracy are emerging in a variety of settings. Some have been inspired and supported by Northern non-governmental organizations (NGOs). Others have grown out of people's collective attempts to secure their economic security – co-ops of craft workers or of farmers and fishers, vendors' associations who democratically set the rules for trade in urban markets. Some organizations have grown up to protect workers' rights such as trade unions or other worker advocate groups. Others spring from churches or mosques where they advocate the welfare of their members and often the broader community. Some are influenced by the ideas of feminism and form associations to fight for gender rights, against domestic violence, or to create income-generating schemes for their members. Democratic groups have also formed to fight for minority or regional rights. Lower caste groups in India and native peoples in the Americas are just two of many such struggles.

A kind of grassroots environmentalism has also grown up in many countries to defend the resources of 'the commons' – water, land, trees, fishing rights, watersheds, air quality – against attempts to privatize, pollute or otherwise expropriate them from public use. This is a particularly important struggle for indigenous people who still depend on the resources of the commons as part of 'a survival economy'. Still other kinds of organization grow out of the margins of desperation. Refugees try and exercise some minimal control over their lives in the encampments that dot Africa and parts of Asia. Street vendors fight against harassment by the police.

The sites and motivations for this kind of local democracy vary widely. But we can find here the flesh-and-blood of a potential strong democracy. For without the self-confidence and personal experience

Strong democracy: liberating minds

Baby Tyawa, an educational psychologist and activist, reflects on the problems of adjusting to freedom and democracy in post-apartheid South Africa.

Things changed here with dramatic speed. During the 1980s we were worried that there was going to be turmoil and confrontation. There is still confrontation now, but of a different type. At that time we were always taking to the streets and I agreed with that. But since 1990, when Mandela was released, I wanted to say: 'Why can't people sit down and talk about the problems we encounter?'

For years repression taught us to resist. Even now we believe we should still be pushing. Some cannot connect the idea of freedom with reality. I recall talking to a union of prisoners and they demanded that all prisoners should be free. And I remember thinking, 'If that's freedom, if that is democracy, then it's a problem.'

The priority is for all citizens to know their rights. By knowing your rights you are then able to understand the limits to those rights. Sometimes we get confused by the mechanisms we use – by 'resistance' we mean taking to the streets. I'm sure we've never known any other way. I think there has to be a concerted program of teaching us how to use other channels to raise our problems, our resistance, in a way that does not stop our advance.

We call ourselves a more democratic society and we should start there, with all the people. It's a process of education. I'd like to incorporate my political ideas within my profession as an educational psychologist. I want to work on our attitudes, our oppressed minds. I think if I don't incorporate my political ideas within my work I'll be missing the point. But I'm not going to lose my political background. ∎

From the *New Internationalist*, issue 265, March 1995.

of democratic practice, demands for popular control are made in a vacuum. Without the sense that self-rule is possible, 'democracy' will be simply more rhetoric from the political class. Without a democratic ethos to infuse political culture, 'democracy' will remain an exotic foreign import from the West unlikely to flower in conditions of desperate poverty and repressive inequality. Such an 'imported democracy' will always be tainted by its association with big power bullying and corporate maneuvering to obtain access to natural resources, exemptions from envi-

ronmental or labor standards and extensive tax holidays. Only practices of democracy that are part of
daily life will prevent it from becoming another ossified hypocrisy used by those with power to trick those
below them.

Brutal resistance

But the struggles to create the local political space for
democracy have proved long and difficult. Resistance
from above has been fierce and many activists have
paid with their lives from Haiti to East Timor. The
brutality of the Indonesian military and its associated
militias in East Timor stands as a kind of template for
the brutality with which undemocratic power and
privilege is defended in the South. Tens of thousands
have died over decades in a struggle to create a self-
determined democracy beyond the reach of the
mandarins in Jakarta. Yet as is so often the case the
heroism of activists in the streets and mountains was
not enough. It took a combination of the political collapse of the corrupt Suharto dictatorship, severe
economic crisis, exceptional international pressure
and solidarity to force the Indonesian military to first
allow a referendum and then eventually withdraw
from East Timor. A democratic impulse from below
usually needs either some encouragement from above
or else an exceptional set of 'crisis circumstances' that
open a space of democratic possibility. It is in such
conditions that there is the chance of building the
institutions of popular power that would guarantee a
strong democracy.

Institutionalizing strong democracy

One place where strong democracy has gained a
foothold is the southern Brazilian city of Porto Alegre.
Here, under the inspiration of the *Partido dos
Trabalhadores* (Brazilian Workers' Party) the municipal
government is organized around a high level of popular participation. As in many Brazilian cities the

municipal budget was subject to the corrupting influence of a traditional patronage machine. A study of local finances in parts of Brazil indicates that as much as 64 per cent of the total budget was misappropriated in this way.

In 1988 the *Partido dos Trabalhadores* initiated a process of popular review of Porto Alegre's budget involving local community meetings at which priorities are set and then further meetings when they are voted on. In the 1996 budget some 100,000 of Porto Alegre's citizens participated in this budgetary process. There are now about 70 cities in Brazil and the rest of Latin America that are trying to develop their own versions of participatory budgeting and planning based on the inspiration of Porto Alegre.

A similar level of strong participation can be seen in the *Panchayat* (an administrative region) empowerment movement in the rural villages of West Bengal. In addition to one of the most radical land reform movements in India, the Left Front Government there instituted a level of Panchayat reform in order 'to increase the opportunities for members of disadvantaged classes (including women and untouchables) to wield public power.' The process included opportunity for budget review and significant local planning powers.[1]

In the subcontinent's south-western state of Kerala, under the leadership of the Communist Party of India, a series of 'development seminars' with around 300,000 participants in 1997-98 taught villagers basic self-governance skills. Ambitious plans called for some 40 per cent of the state budget to be taken from powerful line departments in the bureaucracy and devolved to about 900 individual Panchayat village planning councils. The result has been thoughtful plans with high levels of popular participation in at least some of the villages and an enriching of the democratic process throughout the region with 'the creation of grassroots neighborhood-level groups in hundreds of villages.'

Beyond capturing power

Both the Brazilian and the Indian examples show a tendency towards designing a process of 'people's planning' from below. In both cases these moves can be seen as part of a process whereby traditional centralized (indeed Leninist) Left political parties are reorienting themselves to create organs of decentralized popular political power outside party control. These are both situations where significant democratic impulses from below 'were given life and successfully scaled up and were underwritten by a political project and given state support' – although by state here we are significantly talking about regional and municipal political power. In these cases the parties involved have shifted their ideals from seizing or taking over power to dispersing it in a decentralized democratic fashion.

This contrasts with a number of other situations in the South, quite visible in South Africa, Iran and the Philippines, where powerful and often sophisticated movements helped create social transformations. In all such cases the governments brought to power at least partially through the agency of social movements have then sought to 'normalize' situations and undercut the power of the movements, curtailing their ambitions for a strong democracy. While all these situations are still in flux a pattern clearly emerges of governments either with their own agenda (clerical conservatism in the case of Iran) or subject to the pressures of a neo-liberal global consensus. This neo-liberal agenda (as enforced by the IMF and the US State Department or foreign office) is often adopted as the only course of action or at least the course of least resistance. In such situations the governments quickly moved to monopolize power rather than to disperse it.

The African National Congress (ANC) Government in post-apartheid South Africa for example rules with the good will and overwhelming support of the black population. It has however sought to exercise a technocratic control of the process of decentralization and grassroots empowerment that still exists in its various program documents. Sociologist Patrick Heller notes that: 'Although the ANC was brought to power by a broad-based popular liberation movement, it has consolidated its power through the negotiation phase as the singular representative of the liberation struggle and subsequently through its control of the state. As the electorally-mandated agent of national democratic transformation, and as a party in power, the ANC has squarely rejected mobilization and protest politics as instruments of democratic deepening and development. It has accordingly acted to co-opt or distance itself from its social movement partners, or to transform them into service delivery agents.'[2]

This is a sad judgement on what many throughout Africa had hoped would be an exemplary process of democratization that would shake up the continent's political culture. But it fits with what has happened in many other parts of the South. When power is 'captured' and treated as something to be guarded and protected – rather than extended and dispersed – then democratic possibilities are stunted.

Nationalism replaces democracy

In the Horn of Africa both the Eritrean and Ethiopian liberation movements fought for decades against the brutal authoritarianism of General Mengistu's regime in Addis Ababa. Those who barely escaped the General's 'Red Terror' campaign fled to the mountains and deserts where they slowly built an armed opposition. Their implicit (and sometimes explicit) promise was of a different way of doing politics. Anyone who witnessed the heroism and sacrifice of those years of struggle could not but believe this promise. Years spent living in caves and building schools and factories hidden from marauding MiG fighter jets under the meager cover of the region's vegetation, gave their cause an heroic cast of almost epic proportions.

Yet when these struggles finally bore fruit in a military victory, democracy was slow to come. Power became a 'thing' to be defended rather than a process to be extended and cultivated. As so often in the conditions of fragile nationhood in the post-colonial South, the ideology of the 'nation besieged' replaced a commitment to popular democracy as the glue to hold things together. It was only a matter of years before the two 'liberation governments' in Addis and Asmara were dispatching troops to their common border to renew the slaughter. This time round, the cause was much less noble (some hundred yards of rocky ground plus increasingly obscure national grievances). The euphoria of liberation victory gave way to fear and despair. On both sides the goodwill and hopes of some of the poorest people on the globe were squandered on the altar of nationalism.

One cannot help but speculate what would have happened if the 'post-liberation' period had been devoted to the difficult but ultimately more promising task of extending power to the villages, regions and workplaces of the Horn, as for example President Thomas Sankara tried to do in Burkina Faso before he was assassinated. While this would have been a challenge in a regional situation fraught with tension and distrust, it would at least have been a goal worthy of the hopes rooted in the sacrifice made by so many. Instead we had the familiar rhetoric of 'consolidating the revolution'. It is a situation that has echoes from Hanoi to Havana. As so often in the past, this meant the established leaderships in both Addis and Asmara would cling to power at all costs. In such situations opposition and even criticism are seen to verge on treason. The liberation struggle gets narrowed to the power of a leadership progressively divorced from those who had fought so hard for something different. Without the broader goals and trust necessary for a popular democracy, nationalism becomes the only glue. Sometimes the results are merely an ossification and limitation of a still heroic revolution – as can be seen with Cuba's ageing Castro brothers clinging to power in defiance of Washington. Other times, as in the Horn, it can lead to a slaughter of the innocents.

High stakes poker

So the stakes are high for building a strong democracy in the South. The likelihood of equitable and sustainable development without the institutions of a popular democracy are almost non-existent. Without pressure from below an economic policy based on opening up Southern domestic economies to corporate-led globalization will only increase the inequality and environmental devastation. While some may prosper, most will have their lives uprooted and end up with little to show for it. Their per capita income may increase as they are forced into the margins of the cash economy, but without unions and political organizations to represent them they will remain there. Popular power is needed to shape a society where the wealthy pay adequate taxes, where environmental and labor standards are respected and where collective goods (such as water, housing, cheap public transportation, safe communities and good air) are guaranteed. This will not happen without those who benefit most by it having an effective voice in making sure it does.

Without this kind of strong democracy the South will continue to be plagued by a series of autocratic tendencies generated at least in part by discontents with the corruption and double-dealing of the weak democracy/strong market model. If democracy is simply the excuse for one gang stealing the goodies, other gangs are likely to rebel against it. Democratic alignments then form around regions or groups that feel they simply have been left out and that it is now their turn. Significant policy differences are not part of such a political culture. If a new gang does get in, nothing changes but how the goodies are distributed and to whom. Such a situation also generates pressure to overthrow corrupt (if elected) politicians. Witness the spate of military uprisings that plagued Latin America in the 1970s and still holds on in parts of Asia and Africa today.

More recently the popular reaction to democratic pilfering is religious fundamentalism. This may be Islamic in the Middle East, Africa and Asia, Hindu in India or Christian in Latin America. Such ideologies feed on the corruption and scandal associated with the politics of market democracy. They pit their higher spiritual values against the corrupt materialism associated with 'Marx and Coca-Cola'. The sad choice between fundamentalism and market democracy is well caught in the title of Benjamin Barber's excellent book *Jihad vs McWorld*.[3] The deadly potential for extreme violence and polarization of fundamentalist-inspired movements was made apparent by the cruel mass public executions in New York, Washington and Pennsylvania in September 2001.

The reforming zeal of actual fundamentalist regimes varies greatly, although it almost never includes commitments to extending power beyond a narrow ruling circle who can correctly interpret the scripture of policy.

There is a built-in instability in both the politics and economics of market democracy. Boom-and-bust business cycles. Grab-it-while-you-can politicians. Corporations always ready to move on to greener (less taxes, cheaper workers) pastures. The politics of resentment. Democratic rhetoric used to cloak naked self-interest. A volatile regime of speculation in global financial transactions.

It is understandable, yet odd, that conventional political science is at once obsessed with 'political stability' while it champions the very forces that undermine it. The long-term consequences of these instabilities are too often war and civil war, food short-ages and famine, the mass movement of refugees, bankruptcy and the cutting back of essential services. The same forces are at work in the industrial North although the impacts there are more buffered. A strong democracy, while not guaranteeing stability, would certainly increase the chances. Large sections of the population, with a real democratic stake in the system, would be less likely to be swayed by dema-gogues and the politics of resentment. They would be more likely to defend democratic gains if these were threatened. Strong democracy would enhance the chances for both healthy (as opposed to repressive) political stability and an equitable and sustainable form of development. People would have a chance to insist on it.

1 'Deepening Democracy: Innovation in Empowered Participatory Governance', Achon Fung and Erik Olin Wright, *Politics and Society*, 2001. **2** 'Moving the State: The Politics of Democratic Decentralization in Kerala, South Africa and Porto Alegre', Patrick Heller, *Politics and Society*, March 2001. **3** *Jihad vs McWorld*, Benjamin Barber, Random House, New York 1996.

9 Conclusion

'The job of a citizen is to keep his/her mouth open.'

Günter Grass, German novelist.

Democracy involves risk. This is what is most difficult for many of its advocates to accept, even those who see themselves as risk-takers when it comes to entrepreneurial matters. And democracy is always messy: lots of meetings and reversed decisions. But we owe it to ourselves and the peace of the world to get involved and take on the responsibilities that real democracy puts on us.

WHILE EVERYONE IS in favor of democracy in principle, they want some guarantee that the outcomes will be something they approve of. This is ultimately the logic behind the 'weak democracy/strong market' model. If you take a number of matters out of the hands of democratic decision-makers and instead make them the sole preserve of the market you can limit the impact of unpredictable democracy. There will be no confiscatory wealth taxes, increases in the minimum wage, controls on capital, unwelcome competition from the public sector – if the market is more important than democracy. If you already have money and power this will safeguard you from an 'excess' of democracy that overflows its banks and might wash away some of your property.

But it is not just the self-interested wealthy that worry about the risks of democracy. Many enlightened people are concerned that expanding its scope will lead to an offensive of populist reaction. They fear a generalized assault along a number of fronts: re-instituting capital punishment, outlawing abortion, an attack on gay rights, an end to foreign aid, or defunding social programs through radical tax cuts. These are real fears. But are they enough to place limits on democracy?

It is inevitable that in a strong democracy more issues will become politicized than is currently the case. Under the present model of neo-liberal consensus a great number of what should be debatable public issues have been depoliticized. Whether it is a question of urban planning or of the approval of new pharmaceuticals or agro-chemicals it is assumed to be simply a question of the judgement of disinterested experts.

A more politicized environment with greater citizen capacity to initiate legislation would allow advocates of capital punishment to try and push their case. This is an issue that would need to be battled out. Similarly, introducing more proportionality into the electoral system would allow not only more representation from a principled Left and ecological parties but potentially could allow fascist members of parliament as it does in several European countries. It is hard to see how such risks can be avoided if we want a more profound democracy.

One possibility explored by the French political theorist Chantel Mouffe in her book, *The Democratic Paradox*, is a balance between the strong democracy tradition and that of individual rights rooted more in the liberal tradition of weak democracy. According to this prescription certain rights – say basic civil rights, a woman's right to choose, freedom from discrimination, a sanctity of the person which would preclude capital punishment – would be placed (via a bill of rights enforced by an independent judiciary) beyond the reach of popular decision-making. This would however provide a clear opening for those who would want to place their property rights in the same category. Also, with the political role involved in selecting judges, an independent judiciary cannot be guaranteed. This was made blatant by the intervention of the US Republican-dominated Supreme Court in resolving the

Florida results of the Bush-Gore presidential election in favor of the Republican candidate.

So even if the tradition of strong democracy is qualified by some kind of charter or constitutional guarantee of individual rights this would hardly stop a debate over what rights should and should not be covered. The risk may be modified but it is not removed.

Similarly, a commitment to decentralized decision-making would have to allow local communities and neighborhoods to make decisions that might well fly in the face of accepted norms. This will sometimes result in outcomes that many might regard as negative. Say a community decides under the influence of a powerful real estate lobby to tear down a marvelous old historical building and put up luxury condos. Conservation activists might battle against such a project but in the end wouldn't they be committed to accept the results?

There are several caveats that should be added here. One is that it is far more likely that local people would appreciate the value of an historical building or an unpolluted stream they pass by every day and would want to preserve them. On the other hand a remote industrial zoning board staffed by bureaucrats and political appointees would probably not share that appreciation. Another is that under conditions of a strong democracy where communities get to vote directly on issues it would be necessary to ensure a level playing field. In the case of the fight over whether or not to keep a heritage building, strict spending limits would have to be observed so that powerful interests could not simply 'buy' the results they desired. Access to media would also have to be equalized. A third caveat is that there are some issues of such profound moral weight – say the use of torture by the police or a popularly-sanctioned campaign of ethnic cleansing against a vilified minority – where even a democratically-taken decision would have to be actively resisted.

Another point to keep in mind is that democracy is always messy. Meetings go on far too long. People disagree and march in the streets; sometimes they even throw stones. Everything is questioned. All decisions seem provisional. They may be reopened next week or next decade. People are recalcitrant and stubborn. Things move much more slowly than many feel they should. And then there is all that constant questioning. It is this that offends our managerial sense of things. It is also true that some will inevitably be more active than others. This however will be mitigated by the latent possibility of a more passive majority deciding to intervene once they feel the pendulum has swung too far in a particular direction. In conditions of more localized and direct democracy this will always be an option.

It is necessary not to simply apply the mechanisms of a strong democracy to contemporary situations and prejudices. As Marx warned there is a danger in trying to compose the 'music of the future' in today's circumstances. A society with a high level of self-rule would be built on a citizenship and political knowledge and engagement quite different from that shown by today's passive and often resentful voter. It would occur in a situation of not just more democratic political mechanisms but one where the whole economy and culture is infused with democratic values and practices. This is not to say that all short-sighted decisions and selfishness would be banished (if only!) but simply that they would be more easily *identified* as such, rather than being treated as the common sense of an ethos based on self-interest and might-makes-right.

An ethos of citizenship to replace or at least subordinate passive political consumerism is the only real hope for reviving democracy. The petty resentments and cynicism about all public life spawned by the notion that all politicians (like all brands of Cola) are ultimately the same is a dead end. We need a citizenry that goes beyond blaming politicians and 'throwing the rascals out' to one that takes responsibility for the direction of society. A strong democracy depends on greater equality and on this notion of active citizenship and engagement. This is the very thing that the political class and the journalists, spin-doctors, and opinion-managers who serve it find messy and threatening.

There is an excitement involved with people feeling their own power and gaining confidence in their own capacities for self-rule. Anyone with experience in people running their own housing or food co-op have felt some of this contagious enthusiasm. The possibilities for a generalized self-management have some chance of shifting popular interest from compensatory needs (passive entertainments, consumerism, workaholism, various addictions) to participation in an enriched and empowered public realm. This will of course be a question of degree. But the experience in situations like Barcelona in the 1930s, the Paris Commune of 1871, Hungary in 1956, or the civic engagement in the immediate post-colonial period throughout much of the South gives some grounds for optimism. The altruism brought out by these brief experiences gives some sense of the potential of empowerment in conditions of strong democracy.

A perfect democracy is of course an impossibility. Democracy is in a sense a constant horizon we must strive to reach. Undemocratic concentrations of power will always form and need dissolving. Cliques and cabals will need challenging. Civil service empires will need to be deconstructed. Democracy will never stand still: if it is not expanding it is very likely contracting. As the famous UK historian EH Carr pointed out: 'To speak today of the defense of democracy as if we were defending something which we knew and had possessed for many decades or centuries is self-deception... we should be nearer the mark, and should have a more convincing slogan, if we spoke of the need not to defend democracy, but to create it.'

But how to 'create' democracy? A key to achieving

a stronger democracy is a different attitude towards power. There needs to evolve a pole on the political spectrum around the notion that power isn't just a 'thing' to be captured and wielded for particular policy ends.

A different attitude would see power as something that needed to be dispersed and embedded in everything from workplaces to self-governing communities. While it would still exist at national and international levels, these would no longer be automatically 'superior' to local levels of popular power; rather they would coexist in a complex set of negotiations and checks-and-balances.

A more equal economy with democracy built into the workplace is crucial to this effort. The economy today exerts a constant pull that is used to 'discipline' democracy with what is 'realistic'; to keep some in poverty and others in villas, BMWs and stock options. But even if the essential element of democracy is built into the economy, accumulations of privilege will continue to be an anti-democratic irritant. We'll need to replace our passive consumerist democracy with a reinvigorated polity to provide us with a platform to fight for fairness and equal rights against the blinkered technocrats and free-market globalizers. The inequality generated by the weak democracy/strong market model undermines the mutuality and solidarity between people in society. This inevitably leads to a politics of polarization and resentment between classes, genders, regions and ethnic groups. As we saw in Chapter 8 this is particularly true of the cleavages that are ripping apart political entities across the poor Majority World. To build a strong democracy based on a 'popular sovereignty' that is more than a convenient fiction is the potential beginning of sanity, stability and sustainability. We all know by now what more politics-as-usual will mean.

It may be that democracy will always be unfinished business. But it is *our* business. Let's take it back.

CONTACTS

Australia

Direct Democracy Forum
15 Landry Avenue, Highton,
Victoria 3216. Tel: +61 3 5243 2530.
www.ao.com.au/ddf

Greenpeace Australia
www.greenpeace.org.au/getactive
A broad-based site of news and
networks on community activism.

United Kingdom

Charter 88
18A Victoria Park Square, London,
UK E2 9PB. Tel: +44 20 8880 6088.
Fax: +44 20 8880 6089.
Email: info@Charter88.org.uk
web: www.charter88.org.uk
A broad-based campaign to reform
the centralist Westminster system of
government.

Protect the Local Globally
11 Park House Gardens, East
Twickenham, Middlesex, TW1 2DF.
Tel/Fax: +44 208 892 5051.
Champions of local power and
citizens' initiatives everywhere.

Canada

Democracy Watch
PO Box 821, Stn B, Ottawa, Ontario,
K1P 5P9. Tel: +1 613 241 5179.
Fax: +1 613 241 4758.
Email: Dwatch@web.net

Fair Vote Canada
26 Maryland Blvd, Toronto, Ontario,
M4C 5C9. Tel: +1 416 410 4034.
Email: info@fairvotecanada.org
www.fairvotecanada.org
A movement pushing for electoral
reform and greater proportionality
and fairness in the Canadian
electoral system.

United States

**Center for Voting and
Democracy**
6930 Carro Ave, Tacoma Park,
Maryland 20912.
Tel: +1 301 270 4616.
Email: cudusa@aol.com
Information and strategies on the
malaise of US democracy and how
to combat it.

**The Center for Living
Democracy**
289 Fox Farm Road,
Brattleboro, Vermont 05301.
Tel: +1 802 254 1234.
Fax: +1 802 254 1227. Resources to
rebuild a stronger democracy.

International

**Institute for Democracy and
Electoral Reform (IDEA)**
Stromberg, S-103 34, Stockholm.
Tel: +46 8 698 3700.
Fax: +46 8 20 2422.
Email: info@idea.int
A center that works with Southern
democrats (through an annual
international forum) to build vital and
fair democracies for North and
South.

Movement for Direct Democracy
Bellova 15, Brno 623,00. Czech
Republic. An international movement
that holds semi-annual conferences
to promote direct democracy.
Email: Binka@phil.muni.cz
www.Auburn.edu/tann/prague

Third World Network
228 McAllister Rd, Penang 10400,
Malaysia. Tel: +60 4 226 6728.
Fax: +60 4 226 4505.
Website: www.twnside.org
Coalition of Southern NGOs with an
action, research, publishing focus.
Combines powerful analysis with
effective international lobbying.

On the Web

www.flag.blackened.net/liberty
has a great number of links to anti-authoritarian groups from around the world.

www.australiaconnects.net
creating democracy from the bottom up.

www.democraticinnovations.org
an amazing compendium of ideas to reform and deepen democracy – including links to many other sites.

www.attac.org/indexen.htm
Association for the Taxation of financial Transactions for the Aid of Citizens.

Bibliography

Books

Street-Level Democracy, edited by Jonathan Barker, Between The Lines, Toronto 1999.

Democracy, Anthony Arblaster, University of Minnesota Press, Minneapolis 1987.

Radical Democracy, C Douglas Lummis, Cornell University Press, Ithaca 1996.

The New Challenge of Direct Democracy, Ian Budge, Polity Press, Cambridge, UK 1996.

Journals/periodicals

AMPO: The Japan-Asia Quarterly, PO Box 5250, Tokyo Int'l, Japan; Email: PARC@ca.apc.org Subscriptions $28. Covers the struggle for people's power in Asia.

Review of African Political Economy, Rankine Road, Basingstoke, Hants, RG24 8PR, UK. Tel: +44 1256 330245. Email: sales@carfax.com Covers the blockages both internal and external to the evolution of popular democracy in Africa.

Politics and Society, Department of Sociology, University of Wisconsin, 123 van Deusen, Madison, Wisconsin 53715-2076, USA.

Index

Index